Cioma Schönhaus was born in Berlin in 1922, and lived there with his family until they were deported to extermination camps in 1942. He alone was reprieved from deportation, because of his job in the arms industry, where he successfully sabotaged machine-gun barrels. He was eventually forced to go underground, using his talents and earlier training as a graphic artist to forge ID papers for other Jews in hiding. He received much help from anti-Nazi Germans with this work. However, with the Gestapo on his trail, he made a dramatic escape by bicycle to Switzerland, and this is where he still lives. He completed his art training there and went on to create an advertising and graphic art studio in Basel. He is currently working on the film of this book.

Alan Bance is Professor Emeritus in German studies at the University of Southampton, where he was Head of German for some twenty years. Among his many publications are translations such as *Wild Analysis* by Sigmund Freud (Penguin) and *Winifred Wagner: A Life at the Heart of Hitler's Bayreuth* by Brigitte Hamann (published by Granta Books).

The victor will
never be asked
if he told the
truth!

Nov 12'09

THE FORGER

CIOMA SCHÖNHAUS

With illustrations by the author

Original German version edited and
with a postscript by Marion Neiss

Translated by Alan Bance

Granta Books
London

Granta Publications, 12 Addison Avenue, London W11 4QR

First published in Great Britain by Granta Books, 2007
First published in Germany as *Der Passfälscher*, 2004
This edition published by Granta Books, 2008

Copyright © Cioma Schönhaus, 2004
Translation copyright © Alan Bance, 2007

The publisher would like to thank Pro Helvetia, Swiss
Arts Council for supporting this work.

swiss arts council
prohelvetia

The translator would like to thank the National Firearms Centre
at the Royal Armouries in Leeds for help with some technical
aspects of the book.

Cioma Schönhaus has asserted his moral right under the
Copyright, Designs and Patents Act, 1988, to be identified as the
author of this work.

All rights reserved. No reproduction, copy or transmissions of
this publication may be made without written permission. No
paragraph of this publication may be reproduced, copied or
transmitted save with written permission or in accordance with
the provisions of the Copyright Act 1956 (as amended). Any
person who does any unauthorized act in relation to this
publication may be liable to criminal prosecution and civil
claims for damages.

A CIP catalogue record for this book is available
from the British Library.

1 3 5 7 9 10 8 6 4 2

Typeset by M Rules

Printed and bound in Great Britain by
CPI Bookmarque, Croydon

Contents

Foreword   vii
Translator's preface: A latter-day Scarlet Pimpernel   ix

Heading home   1
Looking like everybody else   3
Prison regulations   8
The death of a tree   12
The drunken policeman   15
Our flat is searched   17
The bomb   19
The decent young Aryan   21
Living like God in France   24
Adam and Evchen   28
A one-year sentence   31
'Degenerate art'   34
Mimicry   36
Berlin Alexanderplatz   41
The waiting room without hope   46
At the lathe   50
The compulsory oath of disclosure   55
Night shift from six till six   58
'Date of deportation: 2 June 1942'   62
The postcard   72
Graphic artist wanted   75
How to forge a stamp   78
Illusions   84
The appendix operation   89
Dr Franz Kaufmann   92

'Just say my name is Rogoff.'   96
Gerda   101
An orderly existence   113
Hunting for rooms   116
The sailing boat   126
Tatjana   130
The Escape Artist   135
Fortune oblige   139
Helene Jacobs   149
Boldness doesn't always pay   157
Betrayed   160
The bicycle   162
A long farewell to Berlin   165
The beginning of the end in Berlin – 6 September 1943   171
Where am I actually heading?   177
My first checkpoint   187
Man proposes, God disposes   193
The forbidden frontier   197

Postscript by Marion Neiss   202
Notes   213

Foreword

My survival is the result of events in which the 'law of large numbers' played the major part.

If the parquet floor of a large room had a hole in it the size of a fist, and somebody tried to land a pea in this hole, his chances of success would be minimal.

But if you took a sackful of peas and tipped them out on the floor, the hole would be filled immediately.

Like mine, the story of every pea that ended up in the hole would then consist of a series of miraculous coincidences. I am one of those lucky peas.

I was encouraged by Professor Heiko Haumann to complete the writing of these memoirs. I would like to thank him for it. Without the great commitment and the constructive criticism I received from my friend Dr Anatol Schenker, and the many discussions I had with him, this book would never have come about. I thank him very much for that. Not least, I want to thank my wife, Rigula, for the great care with which she put the finishing touches to every page.

Cioma Schönhaus

Translator's preface

A latter-day Scarlet Pimpernel

Just as the courage, wit and skill of Sir Percy Blakeney, alias 'the Scarlet Pimpernel', saved aristocrats from the guillotine, so Cioma Schönhaus forged passes to rescue those destined for the gas chambers. But, incredible as it may seem, Cioma Schönhaus's story is not fiction. He was a boy of seventeen when the war began, the only child of immigrant Russian Jews who had moved to Berlin with thousands of other Russians after the First World War. Cioma's father Boris deserted from his Red Army unit to marry Fanja, who gave birth to Cioma (pronounced 'see-oma') in 1922. After a year in Palestine, where they tried to settle, the family rejoined Cioma's uncle and aunt and his beloved grandma in Berlin, where Boris started his own business.

In September 1941, when the story begins, conditions for Jews, although extremely repressive, difficult and restricted, were not yet quite murderous. Cioma was working 'voluntarily' in a labour camp for Jewish youth – in reality, conscripted for forced labour, as was his father. It was still possible to cling to some vestiges of normality and desperately hope that for Jews, things could get no worse. But by the summer of 1942, all of Cioma's relatives had been deported, either to Majdanek or Theresienstadt concentration camps, and he remained alone in Berlin in the family flat, temporarily reprieved by his privileged position as a skilled worker in an armaments factory. Eventually, even this skill could not save him, and he was forced to go underground. The same kind of talent, though, drew him as a graphic artist into a largely non-Jewish resistance network, supplying forged ID documents for Jews living illegally in Nazi Germany. The story of how he became an adept forger, his youthful swagger and courage, even recklessness, his heart-stopping brushes with the Gestapo, his contacts with wonderful German helpers, and the breathtaking episode of his final escape, is not only exciting but also uplifting and moving.

*

Meeting Cioma Schönhaus today in his adopted Switzerland is a great privilege. At eighty-four, he still has all of the gift for friendship, all the charm, optimism, openness, enthusiasm and relish for life that enabled him to seize his opportunities and exploit his incredibly good luck as a young man in mortal danger. There are undoubtedly dark places in his mind, and until this day he has clearly not been able – how could anyone? – to come to terms with that sudden, brutal loss of his much-loved parents in 1942. Starting with nothing, however, he has built up a very good life in Basel, owing great loyalty to Switzerland, whose flag he first saw waving from beyond the deadly Reich frontier in 1943, when it signified hope, sanity and decency. After being so close to this book, I will never feel quite the same again about that chunky white Swiss cross on the red background. Cioma has local loyalties, too; he has written a history of Biel-Benken, the tranquil ex-village suburb of Basel where he has built himself a beautiful house, filled with works of art, mostly by his friends. He is proud to have founded nothing short of a Swiss dynasty. It is significant that two of his four sons are well known for the Klezmer band they have established to play the lively music of the lost Eastern European Jewish communities.

What is most impressive about Cioma is that he is not at all embittered. He travels to Germany frequently, lecturing and answering questions on his book and his life, and when I met him he was working with the ZDF television network on the film they are making of *The Forger*. He has been back to Berlin at least fifty times since he first left the city. He has made his peace with Germany, he says, because of the courageous Germans he was privileged to know when he needed them: above all, the marvellous Helene Jacobs, the woman who sheltered him in Berlin, and to whose memory, as well as that of his parents, his book is unofficially dedicated. Cioma kept in touch with Helene until she died in 1993; she is honoured in the garden of remembrance, Yad Vashem, in Jerusalem, as one of the Righteous among the Nations.

Cioma is still creative and productive, working on a storyboard with hundreds of drawings for the film of his book, and writing the second volume of his memoirs.

Alan Bance, 2006

THE FORGER

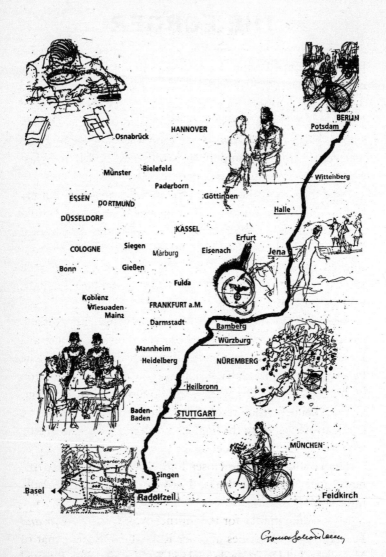

Heading home

It was Friday, 24 September 1941, and I was travelling by express train from Bielefeld to Berlin. For a fortnight I could forget the voluntary work camp of the 'Reich Association of Jews in Germany'.[1] The steam train trailed a banner of black smoke. I kept the windows shut to stop the smuts getting into my eyes. There was a sulphurous smell, hard-boiled breakfast eggs from the restaurant car, perhaps.

I had the comfortable compartment all to myself. I put my feet up on the seat opposite. If the guard made a fuss, I could always shove the *Völkischer Beobachter* under my shoes. I had bought it from the kiosk before boarding the train. It smelled of fresh printer's ink. The front page screamed: BIGGEST BATTLE OF ANNIHILATION EVER. 380,000 RUSSIANS TAKEN PRISONER.

According to the German High Command, the Russian campaign was practically finished. The daily notes of Franz Halder, Chief of General Staff, show that on 3 July 1941 he believed the war in Russia, if not yet quite over, would be won within a fortnight. The *Wehrmacht* dominated the Continent. German soldiers stood resolutely at their posts from the Arctic Circle to Africa, from the Spanish border to Russia, guarding the Greater German Reich.

The conductor came closer and closer. As I pushed the newspaper under my heels, I wondered, 'Is Hitler really unbeatable?'

My reading matter for the journey was Tolstoy's *War and Peace*. Tolstoy describes another Russian campaign, that of Napoleon, who likewise dominated Europe, and also defeated everybody. He, too, appeared all-powerful. But He who limits the skyward growth of trees would ensure there was another

St Helena waiting for Hitler. Whether I would live to see that day was another question, though. For Hitler was not only fighting the Russians; he had declared war on the Jews as well.

When I was a little boy my father often came and sat on the edge of my bed, drumming out the rhythm of a speeding train with his hand on the quilt, and humming at the same time. I could still hear him clearly:

What's going to happen ... don't think about it ... don't think about it ...
What's going to happen ... don't think about it ...

The wheels of the speeding train pounded in 3/4 time, and my father travelled with it.

Mother had a knack of making our two-room flat neat and pretty. White matt-lacquered furniture in the bedroom. Pink curtains at the windows. A crystal bowl full of fresh plums glistened on the dining table. The whole flat smelled of plums.

Next to the dining table, the bookcase: *Das Kapital* by Karl Marx; the *Communist Manifesto* by Karl Marx and Friedrich Engels; *Mona Lisa's Smile* by Kurt Tucholsky. Next to them something by Alfred Polgar, and a few bound volumes of the magazine *Die Weltbühne*. They were all banned books, publicly thrown on to a bonfire in Berlin in May 1933 by howling students during a speech by Reich Propaganda Minister Joseph Goebbels.[2] My cousin had entrusted these books to me before he emigrated to New York, on the express condition that I look after them carefully, since they were irreplaceable.

I found it exciting to eat my supper next to this risky literature. Just having books like this in your possession could prove fatal – if certain people came across them, that is.

There was sourdough bread cut thin, with butter and Swiss cheese. We drank tea with it. And, for me, there was still some of Mama's home-made strawberry jam, to be eaten with a spoon. In Russian it's called *chai s varynyem*.

'So, Cioma, they let you out of prison because the godfather of your non-Aryan girlfriend is a Gestapo boss. For heaven's sake, that's no ordinary event, it's a miracle! But don't rely on miracles. Be careful. Don't play with fire.' All the while Papa was appealing to me to be sensible, he was wetting his index finger, picking up the crumbs from the tablecloth and putting them in his mouth. As he did so he murmured to himself 'thank you'. 'Why are you saying thank you, Papa?' 'Well, you know, it's just my way of saying grace after meals.'

He was working as a navvy at the time, for a civil engineering firm. Fit and bronzed, he explained to me how proper workmen use a shovel: 'First of all, you *never* just use your wrists. And then you have to get the leverage right. That way, this work that was meant to shame us just ends up making me stronger. At any rate, I've never felt better. It reminds me of that book for boys by Mark Twain: Tom Sawyer's punishment was to whitewash his aunt's fence, and on a free Saturday at that. But Tom covered plank after plank, whistling cheerfully, and enjoying himself so much that, as the other boys came strolling by, they paid him to let them paint one plank each.' As some philosopher once said: the way is the goal.

Looking like everybody else

Where the town of Bielefeld ended and the forest began, there stood what used to be a garden restaurant with a large dance floor, dreaming of better days. Above the entrance, a sign read PALACE COURT. Still hanging next to it was a board bearing the legend: WE KEEP OLD CUSTOMS, NEVER FEAR, BREW YOUR

FAMILY'S COFFEE HERE. The building, with its glass veranda, stood in a park planted with old chestnut trees. Three swans sat on a nearby pond. Everything seemed harmonious. But this was deceptive. There were some false notes: the men who had so recently danced here with their wives were now on active service. And by now, real coffee was only available on the black market.

The one true note was struck by us, 120 young men and girls, living in a work camp of the 'Reich Association of Jews in Germany' and working as labourers for various civil engineering companies. It was voluntary work, so far. The Palace Court was designed as a kind of ghetto.

But we didn't want to be ghetto Jews. At the very least, we wanted to look like everybody else – just like Nazis in civilian clothes, in fact. As it happened, there was an old Singer sewing machine under the stairs, on which I tried out what I'd learnt from my mother at home. By backstitching a curved seam I converted my plus-fours into riding breeches. These jodhpurs attracted so much envious admiration in the camp that I was in demand to 'Nazify' numerous pairs of plus-fours. After that, I found a pair of brown officer's boots, in a junkshop flogging ex-army equipment. They had straps fitting round the back of the knees, like polo boots.

One Sunday afternoon five of us were standing in the sun at the garden gate when an old man came down the path. 'What's going on here then?' he mumbled. 'This always used to be a pub, didn't it? Have they run out of beer?' 'No,' said one of us, 'it's not a pub any more. It's a work camp for Jews.' 'Oh, right. That's good. Give 'em what for. I know the Jews. They've asked for it. Put 'em through it good and proper.'

'But we *are* Jews,' I laughed. He ran a glassy eye over our breeches, our highly polished high boots. Then he burped loudly and spluttered: 'Go on, who're you trying to kid? I'm not as drunk as all that.' He staggered off.

In the dance hall of the Palace Court, the balustrades from which anxious mothers once supervised their daughters, had gone. Nothing was left but naked pillars holding up the ceiling, and the art nouveau stucco decoration. Now there was room for fifty sets of grey army bunk beds. At night, when the lads were asleep, the ceiling breathed with them. From a hundred throats the noise intoned, as though from some enormous animal. And yet each one made a different sound.

Michael Kestinger, an overgrown schoolboy, always went around in shorts and high boots. Naked from the waist up, he pointed to his flies and asked dreamily, 'And what is this here?', eyes laughing as Beate blushed.

Walter Majut, a miner from Upper Silesia, blinked in his sleep, as though his miner's lamp gave him too little light. Ludel Frank, a butcher's apprentice, clutched at the air and grabbed a bull by the horns with his sausage fingers. While he slept, Jonny Syna held on tight to the violin case which always lay under the bed. Wolfgang Pander, who always reminded me of the student from Dostoevsky's *Crime and Punishment*, muttered: 'And I'd do it again.'

(One day, Walter Majut and all the other camp mates not mentioned here, were loaded without warning on to a truck. None of them came back. I am one of the few who survived. But that came later.)

Although I was the youngest, and probably the furthest from manhood, I dreamt of getting myself a girlfriend. In fact that was not as unlikely as it sounds. A short while before, Günther Heilborn had put a fatherly arm around my shoulders and asked: 'Cioma, are you blind or are you daft? Can't you see that Lotte is crazy about you?' 'What? Who's Lotte?' 'That one over there, the little blonde with the rimless glasses.' I was afraid of girls. But Lotte was keen on me.

I dreamt that we were drinking sparkling wine and clinking our glasses together: then my glass broke. But it wasn't a wine glass, it was a window pane. 'Pass that hand grenade to me,' hissed someone, 'put the light out!' Something came flying through the hall. Walter Majut and Ludel Frank were in the garden clutching a wooden club and a torch. Out of pure fear, I ran out behind them to see what was going on. There stood the man who had come looking for a beer on Saturday afternoon. Blinded by the torch, he shielded his eyes with his hand. Then he vanished into the darkness. The hand grenade was a brick. And what had come flying into the hall was a wet, empty cement sack. Laughing, but weak-kneed, we made our way back to our bunks.

Lotte had turned my head, but with so many lads in the camp it was easy for her to lose her own. One Sunday we went on an outing to the Arminius monument in the Teutoburg Forest near Paderborn. Lotte was linked arm-in-arm with a boy on each side. Instead of hanging on to laughing Lotte like a spare wheel, I did an about-turn and charged off blindly, headlong across the fields into the countryside. I talked to the sparrows, the daisies and the cabbage butterflies. The sky was blue right to the horizon. The air had a Sunday shimmer. Everything was churning around inside me.

The next thing I knew, a soldier with a rifle slung on his shoulder was saying on the telephone: 'Captain, over here by the ack-ack battery there's a young man walking across the fields. Now he's standing in the shade of the anti-aircraft gun. Yessir. He's wearing riding breeches, English officer's boots. Says he's a Jew, but doesn't look it. Yes, sir, right, I'll bring him over right away.' And to me: 'Come with me.'

The captain sat at his desk, seven officers around him. He turned on his chair to look me in the face through his rimless glasses: 'Young man, have you been sleepwalking? Do you know where you are? You're on a military airfield. Don't you know that nobody's head is safe on their shoulders in

Germany today? I could have you shot out of hand for spying.' He turned to my soldier: 'Take him to the police. Find out what's up with him. If he's in the clear, let him go.' The soldier clicked his heels: 'Yessir!' And to me: 'Come with me!' We marched into the town. 'Would you mind stopping off at the work camp with me?' I asked him. 'My jacket is in there, with my identity card in the pocket. We can clear all this up immediately.' 'Nothing I can do,' he replied.

A quarter of an hour later we stood outside Paderborn Town Hall, adjoining the city gaol. A prison officer opened the big iron gate and looked at us questioningly. 'This Jew has been hanging around our anti-aircraft battery,' began the soldier. 'I'm supposed to hand him over to the police.' In the prison office, I asked the warder taking down my particulars to ring the work camp: 'They have no idea where I am.' The officer acted as though he hadn't heard me. 'Cell five,' he said to the colleague leading me away.

I lay on a hard plank bed. Through the bars of the window I could see a patch of night sky, and I could hear the trumpeter sounding the 'Last Post': 'To bed, to bed, if a sweetheart you have . . .' I had no idea how my father had come to know the tune and the words.

The barracks were right next door to the prison.

Prison regulations

A sign in yellow metal on the wall announced: ANYONE MAKING A NOISE, SMEARING THE WALLS OR DIRTYING A CELL WILL BE PUNISHED BY FORFEITING HOT MEALS OR A COMFORTABLE BED. Aha! So prisoners misbehaving would finish up in a cell like the one I was in, without a comfortable bed. Obviously, all the other cells were occupied.

I looked around. There was another man sitting next to me on the plank bed. Ignoring me, he murmured constantly: '*V imienu oyca syna I svietigo ducha, amen. V imienu oyca syna I svietigo ducha, amen.*' After every 'amen' he crossed himself. I waited for him to pause for breath, and asked: 'Why are you in here?' He turned round slowly and breathed: '*Nie ma pan.*' I had never seen such a painfully thin person. I asked him again. Perhaps he was an Englishman. 'Do you speak English?' '*Nie ma pan.*' Or a Frenchman: '*Parlez-vous français?*' '*Nie ma pan.*' Or a Russian? '*Gavarish pa russki?*' '*Nie ma pan.*' Or a Pole? '*Umiesz po polsku?*' His face lit up, and he began to beam. '*Tak pan tez ż Polski?*' So he was a Pole. He'd been in prison for three months, with no idea why.

The night was hardly over when there was a rattle of keys in the door and a clattering of bolts. You had plenty of warning when they were about to open up, so you could get ready.

A warder with a white, Kaiser Wilhelm moustache ordered: 'Yaroslav Kovaltsek – fold up your blanket. Come with me.' There was no time for goodbyes. What were they going to do with him? Although we had hardly spoken to each other, it was suddenly strangely quiet in the cell.

Before they locked me up, they had made me empty my pockets and hand everything over. A peppermint sweet, a pipe and thirty-six pfennigs. I had pushed my wristwatch all the way up my sleeve almost to the elbow. At first I thought this was really cunning. But afterwards I found out what a torment it was. Minutes pass much more slowly when you can count them. I looked at my watch and exercised my imagination to make the time go faster.

The plank bed was hard. The longer I lay on its bare boards, the more I felt every single bone in my body. For that reason I preferred to walk up and down the cell; it was seven paces long and four wide.

It was exactly ten minutes past eight. In my mind I was strolling through the picture gallery of the Kaiser Friedrich Museum. I had been there so often that I had not only memorized the pictures, but I could remember exactly where they were all hanging. 'OK,' I said to myself, 'first of all you're going to the Rembrandts to look at *The Man with the Golden Helmet*.' I admired the way the white paint, applied impasto, made the decorative pattern on the helmet gleam and shine as the light struck it from the side.

Ten minutes must have elapsed by now. But I clenched my teeth and waited for yet more time to pass; after all, next came the room with those monster canvases by Rubens. And then a detour to take in Vermeer. My God, there was an artist who knew how to paint silk!

While I was admiring Vermeer's work, an elderly gentleman tapped me on the shoulder. He looked like a professor in his broad-brimmed black hat. 'Young man,' he said, 'I've been watching you for some time. And I'm pleased to see a German lad still taking an interest in our culture. Do you know the animal painter Paulus Potter? Come with me: he's hanging over there. Unlike Rubens, he only paints very small pictures. Here, take my magnifying glass and have a look at this cow. He could paint, don't you think? Tell me, are you in the Hitler Youth?' 'No.' 'No, I didn't think so.'

While in my mind's eye I was inspecting Lucas Cranach's slender nudes, the keys rattled in the door again and the bolts clattered. The door opened and the warder with the silver moustache commanded: 'Chamber pots out!' I saw the other prisoners taking it in turns to step up to a toilet. Afterwards, everyone trooped back to his cell with an empty pot. The door was scarcely shut before I was back in the Kaiser Friedrich Museum. Now I finally had time to look at my watch. I had managed to dream myself into the world of art for all of twelve minutes. Smuggling my watch in was not quite as clever as I had thought.

My whole life passed before me as I sat on the bed. My almost nineteen-year-old life. I was never going to get out of here. And my life hadn't even properly begun yet. I hadn't even slept with a woman. And I wanted to have children one day. Was it all over? Was this already the end of the line? Would I be hanged, or shot? Was there a hangman's breakfast for Jews, too? If there was, I wanted sausages and potato salad. Tossing about on the plank bed, I noticed that you could easily pick up a splinter if you weren't careful. The wood was old and dry. But the splinters were good for one thing at least. You could knock up a musical instrument out of this plank bed. A wooden instrument for plucking. And then I could play the merry fiddler and make music before they killed me.

It was quite easy to prise away strips of wood of different lengths, break them off and rub them down thin on the concrete floor. If I wedged them into the gap between two planks, I could produce notes by twanging them. The longer the strip, the lower the note. In that way I could construct a musical scale, which even had semitones. Then I tried it out with nursery rhymes. The time passed more quickly while I was making music. My fears vanished, and I could hear my father telling me a story.

'Just imagine a man falling into a lion pit. Halfway down he gets caught on a root by his braces. The man looks down. Below him vipers are writhing, showing their fangs: above him a lion waits, licking his chops. The man looks ahead of him. There are raspberries growing from a branch that is sticking out. So what does the man do? He eats the raspberries.'

I was twanging the strips of my plank-bed guitar and playing nursery rhymes. They were my raspberries. Then suddenly I was startled by a noise. Outside, in front of the spyhole in the iron door, I could hear someone saying: 'And this is a Jew who was caught near the anti-aircraft post. He's going to be handed over to the Gestapo tomorrow.'

The Gestapo man who came to collect me next morning let me sit next to him in his car. He talked quite quietly. But to me his words sounded like hammer blows: 'Whatever happens to you now, it's all your own fault. You'll be lucky if you only land up in a concentration camp.'

Another Gestapo official, with the physique of a navvy, wrote out a report, and then said: 'Right, now sign that.' As he was leaving the room I began to read through what I was supposed to sign. But the navvy grabbed me by the collar and threw me into the corridor. I was lucky not to fall. He bellowed at me: 'Nosing around in other people's files. It gets better and better. What are we going to do with him?' Luckily, the man who had collected me in his car came past and said quietly to me, 'Come along, come with me', and then out loud: 'I'm taking him with me!' Then he drove me back to the prison.

Next day I had to report to Herr Pützer, the head of the Gestapo's Jewish Affairs Department.[3] I was prepared for the worst. But when I was led into his office, a small friendly man sitting behind the desk nodded his head and laughed: 'So, you're Lotte's friend. My dear Schönhaus, this business could have gone very badly if I hadn't been Lotte Windmüller's godfather. Give my love to Lotte, and tell the camp leader to keep a better eye on his people.' Because of the shock of this arrest I was given leave and allowed to go back to my parents in Berlin for a fortnight.

As a baby, Lotte Windmüller, the daughter of rich, Jewish flourmill owners, had been baptized a Catholic. Her godfather, Herr Pützer, was a close friend of the Windmüller family. The friendly Herr Pützer did his best for his goddaughter right to the end. But even he could not prevent her deportation to Auschwitz. Lotte never came back.

The death of a tree

My leave came to an end. The work camp of the 'Reich Association of Jews in Germany' had assigned us to the firm of Pollmann in Bielefeld, just as though we were ordinary workers.

Although it was early autumn, it was still as warm as summer. Butterflies fluttered over the country road. The asphalt shimmered. No cars for miles, just we three Jewish lads cycling to work: Jonny Syna, a 21-year-old music student, who practised Bach and Saverio Mercadante on his violin in the camp in the evenings; Wolfgang Pander, whose loose tongue had already cost him a couple of months in a concentration camp. Amazingly, they let him out. Before that he had been assistant director in his father's film studio. He was twenty-four. And me: Cioma Schönhaus; after just a year at applied art school, I was nineteen.

The highway was deserted as we rode to Brackwede, a suburb of Bielefeld. We were going to build a static water tank next to a military hospital, for fire fighting. In the distance we heard a truck approaching. It passed us. And then another. On the third one the tarpaulin was half open, and you could see it was carrying soldiers with blood-soaked dressings. They waved, we waved back. 'Look at that!' shouted Wolfgang, 'The trucks haven't got red crosses on them. They don't want people to see wounded men on the roads.'

We cycled between the majestic grey trunks of an old beech wood. The yellow leaves stood out brightly with the light behind them. After about twenty minutes we saw a red works truck parked by the side of the road. The foreman was leaning on his shovel waiting for us. 'So you're my new labourers. We're going to be digging a static water tank here, thirty metres by fifty. My name is Westerfeld-hausen.'

We looked at each other. First we took stock of the patch of woodland with its mighty trunks, and then of the foreman. He was enormous, in a cord suit with a gold watch chain. A head like a mountain climber's, snow-white hair, a white moustache, and blue eyes in a weather-beaten face. You could easily imagine people saying in an undertone at a society party: 'Definitely a lord.' The whole picture changed when he opened his mouth: he had just two front teeth left. But when he called out in his bass voice 'Let's get to work', he was almost a lord again.

We were each issued with an axe. Mine reached almost to my chin. The object was to cut through the tree roots, root after root, until the crown of the tree began to lean in the opposite direction of its own accord. Then, with a rustle of leaves, the giant would lie down, never to rise again. Westerfeldhausen watched me. 'Never used an axe before, eh? I'll show you how it's done. Grab the top of the axe handle with your left hand and let the shaft shoot through your open hand on the right. And then let your breath out loudly when you strike: Haah – haah – haah. That puts some force into it, lad.' My hands gradually became calloused.

'Herr Westerfeldhausen, can I drop out for a moment?' 'Sure.' I had spotted a piece of paper in the forest. There was a whole bundle of them: 'Dear Annemarie, I can understand why you don't come any more', or 'Dear Annemarie, what's happened to your promises?', or 'Dear Annemarie, I don't want you back at all'. The wind had blown them around in the wood; they had no sender's address. Now they lay in the autumn leaves by the hospital entrance.

Our work made progress. The roots of the felled tree, still attached to the soil on the other side, had to be severed. Then, when the branches and leaves were lopped off with the axe, the felled beech lay ready for removal. A lorry brought a group of prisoners in striped uniforms, about sixty men. With a heave-ho they hoisted a tree on to the truck, and then another. We stood by and watched open-mouthed.

Westerfeldhausen shouted 'Breakfast!' and we went off to the works truck. During the breaks I read Thomas Mann's *Buddenbrooks*. Westerfeldhausen glanced at the book, shook his head, and wanted to take a look inside. 'I've never seen anything like it – a workman with a reading book. You'll never amount to anything. Doesn't even know how to hold an axe or fell trees. But reads books! You'll never be a proper worker.' 'Well, I don't want to be one anyway. I want to be a graphic artist and emigrate to America.' 'Yeah, yeah, America. I once had a useless nephew, a real no-hoper, he emigrated to

America. Never heard a word from him since. America, America. All right, back to work.'

I would never have believed it possible that we three lads alone could have cleared and dug a pit measuring thirty metres by fifty. But after three months we had the job done.

The drunken policeman

The Russian campaign in the summer of 1941 was more and more triumphant. There were ever-shorter intervals between the victory fanfares on the radio. The stirring music of Liszt's Prelude was an inspired choice, designed to make you feel you belonged to the strongest nation on earth. Berliners threw open their windows and balcony doors as wide as they would go, so that every passer-by in the streets and squares could rejoice with them. At the end of September the *Völkischer Beobachter* reported that almost half a million Russians had been taken prisoner. Cold-bloodedly, Hitler was to let them starve.

Strangely, while he was enjoying success he left the Jews alone. They even tolerated a Jewish art college in the Nürnberger Strasse. I passed the entrance exam and was allowed to return to school. At that stage I had thought it impossible. I didn't have to go back and listen to foreman Westerfeldhausen telling me 'you'll never be a proper worker'. Now my life consisted of nothing but drawing, painting and girls. And I promptly fell in love with the most spirited of them all: the stepdaughter of the writer Jochen Klepper.[4] The self-confident Renate had intelligent eyes, with a slight squint. She was blonde, delicate and elegant in her movements. But to ensure that her beauty was not perfect, the Lord had given her bow legs.

After school we sat in the Café Quik in Joachimsthaler Strasse drinking something resembling coffee. The place was chock-full. A few tables away from us stood a red-haired policeman without a helmet, his legs planted apart, arms akimbo. His bellowing voice drowned out the general chatter: 'You're a Jew.' The customer he was addressing replied, laughing: 'No.' 'All right, show me your ID card immediately.' The customer was getting angry: 'I said no.' The policeman, now at full volume, roared: 'Out with your identity card, immediately!' Finally, the café manager came over and said: 'Oh, come on, show him your ID so we can have some peace.' The customer gave way. The policeman checked the pass. 'In order,' he said, then put it in his pocket and declared: 'Confiscated!' Like a pickpocket, the café manager retrieved the pass, and the customer put it away. The policeman swayed towards the next table: 'But you are a Jew!'

'Come on, time to go,' urged Renate. I needed no further persuading. We paid and left. In the street we met a policeman on his beat. I went up to him, saluting: 'Heil Hitler, officer! A drunk policeman is pestering the customers up there in the café.' 'What? We'll soon sort that out.' He took the steps two at a time. We stood there hoping he would drag his colleague out into the street by the collar. Sad to say, he came back alone, nodded to me and said: 'Thank you, my lad.' I put my arm around Renate, who looked at me admiringly.

But I could not win her heart completely. I did not stand a chance against her stepfather, whom she absolutely worshipped.

Our flat is searched

Coming home from school one evening, I found my mother kneeling, agitated, in front of the stove, burning a volume of *Die Weltbühne* page by page. 'What are you doing? Are you mad? Those books are irreplaceable. You and your nerves.' 'These books are banned, Cioma. There's been a house search. Gestapo. Do you know what that means? They combed through everything, these books included. I don't know what they were looking for. But Papa has to go tomorrow morning at eight to police headquarters. Isn't that reason enough to be scared?'

Next morning at eight we stood in the corridor of the Berlin police headquarters. On the wall were display cases with photos of drowned people. The stone floor rang when an officer went past in hobnailed boots. A door opened. Papa smiled and signalled goodbye with his eyes. Then the door clicked shut, and the corridor was empty. Further along there was an old wooden bench, worn smooth. How many people had waited here? And for what? We sat down. Time passed. Ten o'clock came. An official walked along the corridor with a heap of files. He needed both hands to carry them. He had to steady the pile with his chin before he could open the door nearby. 'Here,' he called into the office, handing his colleague the mountain of files, 'you deal with this rubbish.' Was Papa's file among them?

Eleven o'clock passed, and Papa did not come back. The police took their lunch break. We walked across the Alexanderplatz, past the Berolina.[5] Mama was biting her lip. Tears were rolling down her face. I gave her my arm, and she took it. I was the man of the family now. We went to the Hackescher Markt district. We knew a Jewish lawyer there, Dr Curt Israel Eckstein. By that stage he was only allowed to call himself a legal adviser, and could only work for Jewish clients.[6] Only he was permitted to enquire about Papa's whereabouts. Nothing reflected his fear more obviously than the way he stood to attention at the telephone as he asked for the Gestapo. He was as curt and clipped in his speech as though he were saluting an officer on the parade ground. Every sentence made him flinch: 'Legal Adviser Curt Israel Eckstein here. I am enquiring about the whereabouts of Boris Israel Schönhaus. Summoned for eight o'clock this morning. Yes, yes, he's staying there. Thank you.' No questions about the reason. No questions about how long; nothing! And then he said to my mother: 'Your husband is under arrest for the time being. I'm sorry, that's all I can tell you, Frau Schönhaus.'

It was like the ceiling of a comfortable middle-class household suddenly falling in. I put my arm around my mother's shoulders. She was a head shorter than me. We went slowly back to No. 33 Sophienstrasse. Breakfast things for three were still on the table. 'There's just the two of us now.' How could I console her?

The bomb

It was painful for my mother that I did not get out of bed when the air-raid alarm went off. The fact that as Jews we were still allowed to use the communal air-raid shelter[7] at Nos. 32 and 33 Sophienstrasse was due to our neighbour's daughter, Gretel Berg. At a tenants' meeting she had asked the block warden: 'Why can't the Schönhauses use the cellar like everybody else? Just because they're Jews? I don't understand that – Jews are people, too.' I wondered whether Gretel Berg would have been so keen to take our part if she had known what went on behind the curtains of the kitchen window opposite, on many a hot summer's day. Instead of doing my homework I stood naked, looking across the courtyard into her open window. When it was warm she wore only knickers and a pinafore. And when she busied herself in the kitchen there was sometimes the flash of a small breast. That was enough. The flash struck me from across the courtyard.

There were air-raid alarms, but nothing happened. Every day my mother started another argument about why I didn't get up. But one night I dreamt that the pianist who lived above us was playing Liszt's *Hungarian Rhapsody* so resoundingly that the walls were shaking, and he and his piano came crashing through the ceiling on to my bed. My mother was shaking me. 'So, Cioma, do you still think there's no need to get up?' We had been hit by a bomb. I hadn't heard a thing. But my mother's hair was suddenly as white as snow.

I was wide awake. Our whole flat was just one big white cloud of old mortar dust. That accounted for the white hair. The bomb had only hit the front of the building, but there were seventeen dead. An old lady was lying injured in her bed in the middle of the courtyard.

What should I grab to take with me? The photos of my graphic artwork. I couldn't think of anything else. Down below on the stairs stood a neighbour. She was the only one in the building who never said hello to us, because we were Jews. When she saw my mother, the two women hugged each other, crying. The other tenants went to the assembly point of the 'National Socialist People's Welfare Service'. They got food there, and blankets, and they were allocated empty Jewish flats, where available.

We went to Uncle Meier's. It was three in the morning. Our footsteps echoed. With practically no luggage we made our way through the blacked-out streets in the moonlight. The gate to No. 11 Münzstrasse was open. We heard Uncle shuffling towards the door. 'Who's that ringing?' Uncle opened up, in his long white nightshirt: 'You? What's going on? In the middle of the night? A bomb, where? How come we didn't hear anything here? Are you sure?' 'But Uncle, our building has been destroyed, we can't stay in our flat.' He was joined by my aunt. 'I'm amazed. It's only two streets away from here. And we didn't catch it at all.'

A new prisoner was brought into the cell block of the police headquarters where Papa was. 'What's new outside?' everyone wanted to know. 'Nothing in particular. Just one of the usual British sleep-busting bombs.' 'Where did it land?' 'In Sophienstrasse. Only one house was hit.' He didn't know which one. 'But only a few people were killed.'

Papa got no more sleep until he was released. Then he appeared at the door beaming, unshaven, pale, a bit thin, but happy to find us all alive. 'It wasn't all that bad at police headquarters. The officer talked to me quite decently, man to man. "We're both adults," he said. "Admit it. It's not going to cost you your head. How much butter did you buy on the black market?"' He had admitted quite honestly: 'About two kilos. "Well, charges will be brought later. But for the time being you're free. Now go home and back to work."'

Papa was sitting at the kitchen table once more, spooning the soup Mama had immediately made him, and telling us the tale of the soft-hearted Gestapo man who wanted to make a Jew happy. 'Every day on his way to the office this Gestapo man sees a Jew, also going to work. Always in the same spot, and always at the same time. The Jew walks bent over, as though carrying his heavy fate like a rucksack on his back. His eyes are sad and half closed. He often stumbles. The Gestapo man is soft-hearted. And he thinks about how he can make this poor Jew happy. Suddenly he has an idea. And next day, when they meet again, the Gestapo man arrests the poor Jew. For no reason. No explanation. Just like that. Terrified, the poor Jew spends a week in the cell block at police headquarters. Nobody talks to him. He doesn't know what's going to happen to him. But at the end of the week his cell door opens; the Jew is free. When their paths cross next day, the Jew passes his benefactor with head held high, whistling happily. And that's how a Gestapo man made a poor Jew happy.'

The decent young Aryan

The year 1941 advanced towards winter. In Russia the temperature fell to 40 degrees below zero. The engines of the German tanks were too cold to start. With their lubricants frozen, the machine guns stopped firing. German soldiers, dressed for a summer Blitzkrieg campaign, froze to death in their thousands. Meanwhile, the Russians sent in winter-hardened Siberian troops. The German Army was stuck in the snow outside Moscow. There was no further talk of a Blitzkrieg. In this situation Germany's allies, the Japanese, hit upon the 'brilliant idea' of a surprise attack on Pearl Harbor.[8] Instead of attacking the Russians from Siberia, the Japanese attacked the Americans. Fortunately. Otherwise, Hitler might yet have won the war.

And just as children building a toy tower feel like kicking it to bits when it goes wrong, so on 11 December Hitler declared war on the USA. He claimed not to believe a 'Judaized' America represented serious opposition. But actually he knew the war was lost. And so he fought – as Don Quixote once tilted at windmills – against the Jews. At least that victory was assured.

One of the first consequences of Hitler's fight against the windmills was aimed at me personally: the Jewish art college was closed down, and I had to report to the Labour Exchange. Jews were only allowed to do menial work, such as digging, or shovelling coal, or dirty jobs in the synthetic rubber industry, where you got completely black and could never wash the blackness off. Unless you were a tailor and could sew uniforms. There was a shortage of such workers.

My mother had been doing forced labour for some time with the tailoring firm of Wysocky. One day she brought home a letter from Wysocky's offering me a job. The official at the Labour Exchange nodded, but gave me a completely different workplace address from the one where my mother worked. She had tried to take me under her wing to hide the fact that I wasn't actually a tailor. What now? I had to report to the uniform makers Anton Erdmann, Berlin Mitte, 6 Poststrasse.

Anton Erdmann himself was a stocky boxer type, who conducted the interview with me in private. What work could I do? 'Everything and nothing. I admit I'm not a trained tailor.

But my mother is a dressmaker, and I've often helped her. I'm sure you could find a use for me.' Anton Erdmann looked at me thoughtfully. 'Do you know what? You don't look at all Jewish. I'll employ you in the Aryan department. You are my assistant and your name is Günther. Your job will be to distribute trimmings to my ninety-six Jewish tailors – buttons, braid, insignia and so on. You'll be in charge of the small stockroom, and answerable to me. Our agreement remains confidential. Got it?' The Jewish tailors were enthusiastic about the decent young Aryan.

'Although the name may sound all right, it's always just the same old shite,' said a text in fancy Gothic script, written on a postcard on Hans Schabbehard's office wall. He was my boss: the second most important man in the firm. He was about thirty-five. Hans Schabbehard had been in the army for a while. Eventually they had discharged him because he was half Jewish.[9] It had not affected his good humour at all. Always cheeky, always whistling as he made his sprightly way along the corridor, always tapping out rhyming slogans: 'Rare is the merchant you can make, Crap instead of goods to take', or 'If your lampshade's full of shite, Then the shop will have less light'. He took a fatherly interest in me. He didn't want me taking up with the glamorous Wilma, because that would be a 'racial offence'. But once, when 1,000 marks disappeared from the office, he stuck his neck out for me: 'Günther wouldn't pinch anything.'

Anton Erdmann had bought a sailing boat. It had to be moved from Wannsee to Pichelsberg. Schabbehard sent for me: 'Günther, you're coming along!' For the first time, I felt what it was like to be carried along by the wind, gliding over the waves and being transported gratis by the good Lord; I resolved to take up sailing later.

Living like God in France

The doorbell made a creaky sound. Through the peephole I could see a German soldier. I opened up. Before me stood a captain in his Sunday-best, walking-out uniform. 'Can I come in?' He was carrying a large parcel. 'First of all, best wishes from Adi Berman in Paris.' Mama's eyes widened as she declared: 'That's my brother.' 'Yes, I know, and he's told me a lot about you, and about his nephew.' He looked at me: 'Is that you?'

He took off his cap, laid it on the kitchen table and undid his coat. 'It's well heated in here.' He was still standing; Mama didn't dare offer him a chair. 'Adi and I are good friends. He's what you might call my business partner. I'm a purchasing officer for the German Army. We go out a lot, to Maxim's, or the Folies Bergères, and of course his wife, Suzanne, always goes with us, a really charming person, by the way.' He put the parcel down on the table. 'He's sent you this,' he said, and without a by your leave he began to open it, producing a giant bottle of Hermès Eau de Cologne, Cuisenier Liqueur, pralines, real coffee, silk stockings, chocolate and a letter: 'Enjoy yourselves,' it read. 'The bearer is a good friend. If you need anything, just let him know. He comes to Berlin once or twice a month. His name is Paul Albrand.'

The German captain put his cap back on. 'I'll give you my visiting card. It's got my telephone number. I live at 267 Kurfürstendamm.' And then he was off. By now Grandma, Aunt and Uncle were in the kitchen, too. We all looked enquiringly at each other. What was all that about? 'Typical of Adi,' mused Mama. My reaction was: 'Right, let's go and visit Herr Albrand. He can take me to Paris with him.'

I wouldn't give up. And two days later I was sitting on the

My portrait of Grandma

underground with Mama, heading for the Kurfürstendamm. The carriage was almost empty. Mama sat opposite me. We played the old game of 'who can stare longest without laughing'. Our eyes were absorbed in each other's. At the same time, Mama was biting the inside of her lip and pulling her mouth out of shape, so that little wrinkles appeared on her nose. I couldn't hold out any longer. She won.

Paul Albrand lived in the exclusive west end of Berlin. There were six steps from the street up to the main entrance. Next to it there was a small white enamel plate that said in black letters: ENTRANCE FOR GENTRY ONLY. We went into the building, passing on our right the little window from which the concierge could watch who came and went. Then we climbed the marble staircase, the red carpet runner that extended right to the top, absorbing our footsteps. On every floor we saw different-coloured, leaded, bull's-eye panes. It all reminded me of a church.

Paul Albrand opened the door to us dressed in civilian clothes, looking a bit like an Italian film star. He ushered us in. In the haze of cigarette smoke a stupefying perfume hung about the room. In one corner, a blonde girl lounged on a sofa, her legs in black stockings, her feet propped up against the wall, her long hair tumbling on to the carpet. She acted as though we were not there. Albrand joined us at an occasional table. 'Well, all I can say is that right now in Paris you can live in clover, literally "like God in France", as the saying goes. I do the purchasing for the *Wehrmacht*, and Adi knows all the good addresses. We scratch each other's backs.'

Mama was sitting on the edge of her stool, like a child on a visit. She kept on looking at the girl, and then at the clock on the wall. She wanted to go home. And I wanted Albrand to take me with him to Paris. To that great freedom, as I thought of it. He nodded at me: 'Why not? Just let me think. If you can get hold of a square-section key, perhaps . . . I've got an idea. The doors on the outside of the railway wagons are locked with a square-section key, and if you squat down on the step of the wagon when you get to the border, you can practically get by without being checked at all. That would be quite something, eh?' I was dead keen, and already wondering where to buy a square-section key. He told me to ring him in a fortnight.

Mama was beside herself – she thought the plan was far too dangerous, and didn't like the idea one little bit. I did.

As soon as I could, I went to a tool shop. 'I want a square-section key, please.' The salesman brought three: 'What size do you want?' 'I'll take all three of them, they're not dear.' Now I had to try them out. The Anhalter station was full of people. That suited me. But hardly had I sorted out the right key, when I heard a voice behind me: 'Check on foreigners, all passes to be shown!' That was all I needed. My ID card said 'Cioma Israel[10] Schönhaus', and I wasn't wearing a Star of

David. All the conditions were right for getting myself arrested. I stood as though rooted to the spot. 'Your identity card?' I looked in all my pockets. 'Where the hell is it?' The man in the trilby hat, typical Gestapo, was waiting. I was still searching. What should I say to him? I'm not a foreigner, perhaps; or, I'm not travelling at all; or, I just came to see my girlfriend off at the station; or . . . But he didn't question me – he had already moved on to the next carriage.

There was enough room for a church tower in the station concourse. An engine puffed out clouds of steam, which collected in the glass roof. The echo returned the sound twofold. I still hadn't moved from the spot. In the distance I could hear: 'Check on foreigners. Passes. Your passes please.' And then from further away: 'Check on foreigners.' I moved slowly down the three steps from the wagon to the platform, and strolled towards the exit stairs. Steam issued from the restaurant car galley. I sauntered as though in no hurry. In my head I heard: 'Cioma, listen: you need an Aryan ID card, not one with the name "Israel" on it, but one that says you're not a Jew.' Once in the street, I rushed home. The message hammered in my head: 'A pass with no "Israel", with no "Israel", with no "Israel".'

It was already dark. Everybody was asleep. Then the door opened quietly: 'Cioma, do you know the time? What are you up to?' My mother, in her red dressing gown, picked up the pass from which I had just scraped away the word 'Israel' with a razor blade. 'For God's sake, you'll get into trouble. You'll get us all into trouble. Throw your pass away, and I'll report to the police station tomorrow that you've lost it.' 'That's a good idea, Mama. Do that. Report that it's lost. But I'm keeping the pass without the "Israel" all the same.' Sobbing, she went to bed. I sat down on the edge of her bed and took her hand in mine: 'Mama, I want to live, I want to get out of here.'

The fortnight was up. Albrand never picked up the phone. I dialled his number again and again. I waited another week. But it was no good; nobody answered.

In the end I went to the Kurfürstendamm. In front of the building, in a green space, there was a telephone box. I tried phoning him from there. Suddenly there was a crackling on the line and a female voice asked: 'Do you want to get to know me? If you open the door of the phone box and come out, you'll see me on the third floor of the building opposite, on the balcony.' I stepped outside and looked up. A young girl was waving. I signalled to her to come down. 'Yes,' she said, 'I often do that. From the balcony I can always see who's phoning from the box. And if I want to pick up somebody I like the look of, I just dial the number of the phone box. I've got to know some great people that way.'

Close up, I didn't find her pretty at all. But her balcony was on the floor where Albrand lived. 'Do you know Herr Albrand?' 'Oh, him? Didn't you see it in the paper? He's just been convicted of black marketeering and executed.' I thanked her for the information and walked back in a daze, along the Kurfürstendamm to the underground station. At home, Mama said: 'What did I tell you? I never liked him from the start. The people Adi does business with! I hope nothing's happened to him.'

But I had made up my mind: I wanted to get out. Only I didn't yet know how.

Adam and Evchen

Anton Erdmann had shoulders like a wardrobe. His eyes looked somewhat Mongolian, and his skin was like someone who had recovered from jaundice. Bursting with energy, he always had to keep the corners of his mouth under control because a laugh constantly hovered on his lips. He knew all of his ninety-six Jewish tailors by name, and was always ready to tap out a cheerful slogan on any available surface.

One morning, he greeted everybody at eight as usual; the sewing machines began to whirr, and then, ten minutes later, the big entrance doors swung open again. Somebody had arrived late. Erdmann's brow furrowed, and he pointed to the clock on the wall. The latecomer asserted quite confidently: 'That clock is ten minutes fast.' Erdmann did not hesitate for long. 'OK, no problem,' he said, and taking a key, he turned the hands back ten minutes. Everybody groaned, but Erdmann grinned and remained unmoved. The latecomer sat down red-faced at his machine, knowing that because of him ninety-five colleagues would have to work ten minutes longer. All the same, everybody was nice to him at lunch hour. A few seemed to be suppressing a laugh, however. At six o'clock it suddenly became clear why. Some joker had unpicked the sleeves of his overcoat. Goodness knows how long it took him to sew them back on again.

The next day Anton Erdmann called me into his office. He pushed aside a chair to shut the door properly; it was usually open all the time. 'Günther, it's impossible for a normal person to grasp what our soldiers are doing to the Jews in Poland. God help us if we lose the war. We'll all be for it. But in the meantime, you people are catching it. Günther, you're going to have to wear a star[11] like everybody else. And I can't keep you down here with the Aryans any longer. I'll help you get into the firm your mother works for. They've got better connections at Wysocky's. You'll be safer there. The old Jewish owner is still the boss, on the quiet. They can't do anything without consulting him. Over there they have a better line to the top. How it works, I have no idea. But they can do more to protect you at Wysocky's. I'm afraid I'll have to get somebody else for my Jewish tailors. But please keep this to yourself.'

Proudly my mother presented me to her workmates. The Jewish former boss, Walter Prager, could easily have been an American general. With his bass voice he would have made an ideal radio announcer. Nobody said no when he wanted anything. Not even the new factory owner, Herr Wysocky. (If Walter Prager had not worn his star, nobody would have guessed he was Jewish. Even now in heaven he is probably somebody special. In the Jewish cemetery in Berlin Weissensee, where the millions of murdered Jews are commemorated, there's a white stone by the edge of the path that cannot be missed: Walter and Nadja Prager.)

Walter Prager also impressed me because as well as his pretty wife, he had an even prettier girlfriend in the firm, Evchen Hirschfeld. One of the tailors – a former music-hall artiste with a whistling act – said once, as Evchen stood next to him between two clothes racks: 'Evchen, you'd better move away from here, before something comes up between us.'

For some unaccountable reason Evchen suddenly became my mother's friend. She used to come home with us after work. Mama always managed to conjure up something tasty, despite the food shortages: liver dumplings made of oatmeal, Russian cabbage soup (borscht) with tomato purée, or fruit loaf made with potatoes. But Evchen ate practically nothing, and spoke very little. The only thing she did like doing was showing off her teeth at every opportunity. Why she did so was a mystery. Her visits didn't seem to have anything to do with me.

One night, when the curfew hour for Jews had long since passed,[12] Mama had already said good night, and Uncle, Aunt and Grandma were asleep, only Evchen stayed on, leafing through an illustrated magazine. I knew that at any minute somebody might come in and cross the room to get to the lavatory. But I didn't care. My mind was in a whirl as with trembling fingers I began to open Evchen's blouse. 'There are a lot of buttons,' I heard Walter Prager saying. But from one button to the next his bass voice became quieter, until he fell silent in the mist.

Our clothes were lying on the floor. We crouched next to them like Adam and Evchen. I didn't know what to do, but Evchen did. Hardly had I become aware what was happening before it was all over. The couch cover can be cleaned, was the thought that shot through my head. Evchen began to dress slowly. I wanted to see her home, but she declined.

Next morning during the break she was sitting next to Walter Prager again. I nodded to her, but she looked right through me. She stopped coming to us in the evenings after work. When Mama asked what was wrong, I just said: 'Nothing, why?' But inwardly I fell into a deep pit. Lying on yesterday's couch cover, I made myself a small boy again by shaving down below. It was itchy in the mornings, but it seemed to pre-empt the danger of going through anything like that with a girl again. I could not show myself to anyone in that state.

A one-year sentence

Next morning there arrived, plain and cold, a summons to court for Papa. It could only be to do with the butter. 'It won't be all that bad,' the officer at police headquarters had said.

Papa, Uncle Meier and I went in bright sunshine to the courtroom. Uncle found the last free seat in the gallery. Then they shut the door. I was left outside. The corridor of the court building was a symphony of red marble and white limestone, with mosaics here and there. The judges in their black robes put the finishing touch to the setting. I stood in this grand corridor and waited. I fiddled restlessly with the handle of another door. It opened. Behind it I could see a spiral staircase with iron steps, and walls of rough brick. Good enough for convicted prisoners on their way to the cells or the scaffold. Although it was certainly forbidden, I walked down a few steps to a narrow door. Through a gap I could see into the courtroom. The judge's tone of voice froze the blood in your veins. Every word the accused used in their defence, he imitated mockingly in a nasal Yiddish intonation. Without warning, the judge called the court usher. 'Is there somebody behind the door to the prison wing? Bring them in here immediately!' I was quicker. Escaping arrest, I strolled to 11 Münzstrasse, deep in thought.

It was dark by the time Uncle got home from the public gallery. My mother looked at him enquiringly. And he – who used to be a trumpeter in a Russian military band – raised his hand, as though to give a signal like a conductor. Then he shrugged his shoulders helplessly. 'A year,' he muttered. The silence in the room was shattered by a primal scream. Prison was a category of punishment which was inconceivable in a respectable Jewish household – even by that date. But there was nothing to be done about it. I lay down on the bed next to Mama with my shoes on and tried to comfort her. 'You've got a girlfriend, Cioma. But my friend is in prison.'

I had been given a present of a packet of cigarillos by a colleague at work. I inhaled the tobacco aroma along with the cool morning air. Passing the houses of the Prussian aristocracy on my way to work, I made believe I was a Prussian prince who was fighting Hitler in the resistance. I didn't want to be a Jew. I lowered my own private iron curtain.

Soon afterwards I found the right girlfriend, Dorothee

Fliess. She wore a tartan skirt whose pleats showed off her legs at every step. She was one of the best hundred-metre runners in the school. When I asked whether she would go canoeing with me in the canoe I inherited from my cousin, she tossed her hair back jauntily and said: 'Why not?' And the following Sunday we paddled across the Wannsee together.

Actually our friendship was a mismatch, because as German Jews saw it, Jewish and Gentile Germans had more in common than German and Russian Jews. My new girlfriend's father, Dr Julius Fliess, was an eminent lawyer and a German Jew through and through. He was commissioned in the First World War. That was unusual; as a rule, German officers came from the aristocracy. If a commoner, especially a Jewish one, became an officer, he had to doubly fulfil the ideal of the dashing Prussian officer. When Julius Fliess was badly wounded in action and lost an eye, he reported for duty in the trenches again the moment he had halfway recovered.

My father was just the opposite: a typical Russian Jew. He, too, had been a soldier, but in the Red Army. And not for long. As soon as he became company clerk, he started planning to desert with his captain, an old school friend. And not for any political reason: no, simply because he loved his girlfriend, my mother, and wanted to get married. The concept of patriotism was foreign to Russian Jews. Whenever there was a government crisis or a military defeat, pogroms served to deflect popular anger away from the regime. That hostile environment made the Jews retreat into close family circles, and produced a good deal of warmth and humanity.

When I told Dorothee that my father was in prison, she shook her head: 'You know, Cioma darling, that's the kind of thing that could only happen to you.'

'Degenerate art'

Dorothee and I were taking a walk one Sunday morning along Grossadmiral-Prinz-Heinrich-Strasse. It was Sunday weather. We looked as though we were on our way to the tennis court. Her blonde hair could be seen from a distance streaming in the wind; what could be more Aryan? Our yellow stars were invisible, tucked away in our pockets. We had unpicked them and fixed press studs to the back. That way, they could be removed and fixed on again at will.

On one side of the street, cast-iron railings ran along the Landwehrkanal, the canal where they found the body of the murdered Jewish revolutionary, Rosa Luxemburg. On the other side were upper-class villas with their trim front gardens, here and there adorned by the oval plaque of an embassy with its national coat of arms. Suddenly I spotted a brass plate that interested me, as a student of graphic art. 'Gallery. Exhibition open until 12 noon.' 'Come on, we're going in here.' After we had been looking around for a while, a man appeared at the entrance, tall and slightly stooped, probably because most people he talked to were shorter than him. His narrow head, fringed with white hair, inclined to the left as he surveyed us over his glasses. The last visitors had left. 'Excuse me – I have been watching you for some time, and I'm pleased to see that there are still young people interested in art.'

He shut the entrance door from inside. 'It's past twelve o'clock, anyway. I was listening with half an ear to what you were saying earlier about the pictures on show, and I could tell that you are an artist of some kind. I'll show you something now. Just come with me.' He pulled back a curtain. 'Do you know what that is? A genuine Pechstein; over here is a

Nolde, and this is a picture by Beckmann. The best German artists are banned from painting today. They call them "degenerate" because they don't paint as naturalistically as our Führer would like. It makes you laugh, but most modern German artists keep something representational on hand in case they need it. An apple or a flower painted naturalistically. The Gestapo have nothing better to do than inspect the studios of modern artists. Anyone painting "degenerately" risks going to a concentration camp. It's a terrible shame that our Führer was once a painter. Now he thinks he's an expert on painting, too.'

He went on to show us a Kokoschka, and then began to grin: 'An amusing thing happened to me recently. I have an aunt who paints as a hobby. Such things can occur in any family, and for the sake of peace I couldn't refuse house room to a couple of her wretched flower paintings. I tucked them away in a corner at the back. And guess what happened – two gentlemen from the Reich Propaganda Ministry came along, looking for pictures for the Führer's Reich Chancellery, and with the unerring instinct of connoisseurs they picked out my old aunt's pictures. I couldn't believe my eyes. Yes, we live in great times. Have a nice Sunday.' We walked home thoughtfully.

The blackbirds went on blithely building their nests, while the corpses of German soldiers frozen to death outside Moscow were slowly thawing. There was no longer any prospect of winning the war. All the same, the 1921/1922 age groups were sent towards the Russian guns, and the few hundred thousand deaths that resulted were deemed acceptable.

The Führer of the German Reich was a vegetarian. Although his guests could order meat dishes if they liked, at dinner he referred to them as corpse-eaters. Hitler did not eat corpses; he just created them, by the million. He was not stupid. He just uncontrollably despised humanity, and lied to it. And with his lack of compassion he was a virtuoso liar. First of all he deceived his political opponents, then the German people, then the whole world, including the Jews, before they died.

At the beginning of April 1942 the victory fanfares proudly announced: 'Results achieved by our navy and the *Luftwaffe* in February and March: 41 enemy warships sunk.' What the victory fanfares did not announce, however, was that in that year the Americans built 5,339,000 tonnes of new shipping. So the half-truth was in fact a complete lie.

Mimicry

One Saturday in the summer of 1942 Dorothee and I took a trip to Fangschleuse, a spot popular with Berliners, just outside the town. She was twenty and I was nineteen. I had just specially cleaned up and oiled my cousin's rickety old bicycle. We pedalled along silently side by side. Jews were forbidden to cycle,[13] but there wasn't a policeman or a car in sight. Only the scent of lilac accompanied us and the pounding of my heart, after she said: 'You know, Cioma, you can never tell what the future holds. But if we get torn apart and I ever see you again on the other side of the street, I will still be as crazy about you as I am now.'

There was a room to let in a farmhouse. The farmer's wife showed it to us: 'Nice and sunny, eh? There's only one bed, but you are brother and sister, after all. Where have you come from?' 'From Berlin.' 'What? Then you must have seen our Führer. Just a minute!' She came hurrying back, carrying a plate of home-made cheesecake.

We sat on the edge of the bed eating our cake, completely alone for the first time. Dorothee looked at me sadly. 'I'm going to tell you a secret. But for God's sake keep it to yourself: I shouldn't be telling you this at all. Can you believe it, next week I've got to emigrate to Switzerland with my parents. But I'd much rather stay here with you, in my lovely Berlin.' The cake almost stuck in my throat. I was appalled. 'How can you manage that?' I asked. She told me no more details, just begged me not to mention the emigration plan to a soul.

(Many years later I heard the story of Dorothee's father. He knew Hans von Dohnanyi from the time they spent together in the Reich Ministry of Justice. Quite early on, Dohnanyi – already a Specialist Officer in Foreign Intelligence – and his superior officer, Admiral Wilhelm Canaris, had made contact with the army officers' resistance movement. These two men had managed temporarily to hold off the deportation of the Fliess family among others, and early in the summer of 1942, Dohnanyi was looking for some way to get them all out of the country. Then, in a discussion Dohnanyi had with Canaris and Himmler (Reichsführer of the SS and head of the German police) it emerged that the latter was considering using Jews as agents abroad. Himmler demanded that his plan be put into operation, and finally a group of Jewish people was assembled, including the Fliess family, to be sent to Switzerland.)[14]

In the Wysocky workshop, forty-eight women and four men were backstitching, piping, lining and trimming field-grey *Wehrmacht* uniforms. The goods were checked in a small adjoining room and then the uniforms were sent off to the army outfitting depot.

Det Kassriel, a workmate a bit older than me, got on well with my mother. He was a real, trained tailor. He could sit cross-legged on the table and trim a hand-sewn seam on an officer's collar in overlock-stitch. His fingers were always a little bit sweaty, but he could bend them in all directions, like rubber. After work he often used to go to the covered market, where the stout market women were his customers: he tailored two-piece suits for them that made them look slimmer. He didn't work for money, but for bacon, sausage and cheese.

His face somehow reminded me of a little sailor, and he had two real sailor friends, Aryans. 'Cioma, are you coming to the Kaiserhof?' 'Me?' 'Yes, you!' 'Are you mad, Det? Do you know what the Kaiserhof Hotel is? That's Hitler's local. That is where Goering brought him the news that he had been made Reich Chancellor. It is where Kaiser Wilhelm held his gentlemen's soirées for deserving officers. It's where Bismarck lived before he moved into the Reich Chancellor's palace. And that's the place where you want me to spend an evening with you?' 'Yes, of course, that's exactly why! Do you think anybody asks Goering, Himmler or a Prussian prince for their ID? As long as you look confident, you can't go wrong. Anyway, there'll be four of us. My sailor friends are coming with us in their navy uniforms.' 'Det, you're crazy. Why do you do these things?' 'You know, Cioma, when Wysocky's delivers uniforms to the army outfitting depot, I take the delivery book and sit next to the soldier who drives the truck. Just the other day, the driver seemed almost to be talking to himself, but anyway he told me that the chimneys in Poland are belching smoke day and night. They're burning all the Jews, Cioma, and it'll be our turn one day. But I'll tell you one thing – they won't get me. I'm not going: I'll go into hiding in Berlin. I'm practising moving confidently in Nazi society, so that I don't look like a frightened Jew. In the animal world it's called mimicry. Now, are you coming with us or not?' Naturally I went.

The livery of the flunky by the revolving door gleamed with gold braid. The general who was just going in looked distinctly modest by comparison. A barman with military-style cropped hair shook his cocktail mixer and enquired: 'What would you like, gentlemen?' Det suavely ordered whisky and soda, four glasses, no ice. I perched with one buttock on the bar stool. One of the sailors told us about a night attack in a fjord, where they rammed and sank a British torpedo boat. Two men listening nearby were impressed. I didn't see any women at the bar. Or maybe I didn't notice them because my heart was pounding so fast. But outwardly I was the complete Prussian prince on leave in mufti.

It got closer to midnight, and I knew Mama would be worrying. Because of the blackout in the city, we walked in step through the streets four abreast, arm in arm, so as not to lose each other. The façade of the new Reich Chancellery was built on a scale that seemed to threaten mere humans. It took ten minutes to walk past it. Next to the massive granite stones you felt particularly small. Black and menacing, the building lay there sleeping, like a savage animal, ready to pounce.

I woke up late with sunshine pouring into the room and the bells of St Sophia tolling in the distance. The doorbell rang and Mama opened up to a Sunday morning visitor. A woman of about fifty stood at the door. 'Good morning, Frau Schönhaus, I hope I'm not disturbing you. My husband is a prison officer in Tegel gaol, where your husband is.'

Mama didn't know what to say. She invited the woman in and offered her a cup of tea. 'It's like this, Frau Schönhaus: my husband supervises the prisoners. They have to sort out the waste on the sewage farm outside the city, where all the rubbish from Berlin ends up. Well, guess what, your husband recently came across a whole consignment of rotting geese. He reported it to my husband, and told him that he could make good hard soap out of them if he could find the right chemicals. My husband managed to get hold of the stuff, and look what yours made with it.' She produced a bar of hard soap from her shopping bag. Soap like that was worth its weight in gold at the time. The whole kitchen began to smell of soap.

'The two men have almost become friends, Frau Schönhaus, so you can go and visit your husband now and then, without a visitor's permit. And the boy as well. But first your son will have to come to our place and go over the details with my husband. This is my address.'

Later, when I got to Tegel as arranged, the warder himself opened the big black door to the small branch prison. The only people held here were the twenty-two prisoners who worked at the sewage plant. The warder greeted me like an old friend, put his arm round my shoulders, and took me into his office. The other officers watched. The business of the arm round the shoulders had been pre-arranged in his house. And who should be standing in his office? Papa! Tanned, and still wearing his Stalin moustache. His eyes caressed me, and we hugged each other. 'Papa, it's so lucky that you're in this little outbuilding. You could escape from here.' 'For God's sake, Cioma, what are you talking about? And anyway, where's your star?' 'In my pocket. That's what I arranged with the warder; otherwise I couldn't have got in here at all.' '*Cioma, nye rush nichevo, nye boysa nikavo.*' (Don't make trouble, then you don't have to be afraid of anybody.) 'Papa, do you know what's going on here? They're sending all the Jews to Poland and they're killing them there. We should get out while we can!' 'Don't talk nonsense. What you're saying is impossible. They can't kill all the Jews. But it worries me that you're going around without a star. Please phone the warder to let me know that you have reached home safely.'

The tailoring workshop at Wysocky's smelled of peppermint tea and real coffee. God knows where Walter Prager got hold of the coffee.

In the pressing room, Paul Levi, the buttonhole-maker, and Karl Wiesner, the presser, sang soldiers' songs from their glory days, a time when they were equal citizens of Germany in the trenches of the First World War. I sang along with them:

And if a bullet shoots me dead and home I cannot wend,
Then do not shed too many tears, but find yourself a
     friend.
Take care to find a fine young lad, my lovely Annemarie.
And I won't mind if you don't find
One from my Company
One from my Company.

Or sometimes it was:

Stand fast, stand fast in the storm's deadly blast
So the world can see, the world can see how loyal we can be.

Berlin Alexanderplatz

No. 11, on the corner of Münzstrasse, was only a few min-utes' walk away from the Alexanderplatz. It was a six-storey, red brick building with a bay window at the corner of every floor. Uncle Meier sat at the window on the fifth floor, his elbows propped on the windowsill, watching the scene below. To the left, in Rochstrasse, market wholesalers began shouting at about five in the morning, negotiating their prices. Boxes of tomatoes, apples, pears, strawberries, oranges, mushrooms, carrots, cabbages, plums and potatoes were offloaded, to be sold in the greengrocers' shops. By eight the whole hullabaloo was over. Then it went quiet. All that was left was the typical covered-market smell of rotten tomatoes, picked over by homeless women to see if they were still edible.

On the other side of the Münzstrasse a jeweller's window full of watches, rings and diamonds radiated a picture of peace. Before the war peroxide blondes in high heels, with short skirts and red leather jackets, used to saunter along here. Now the 'German woman' worked in the munitions industry. She did not use make-up. She did not smoke. She only ever demanded a holiday in order to give birth, if at all. Just the same, as Uncle watched from his window, negotiations took place opposite and inconspicuous women disappeared into the hotel on the corner, arm-in-arm with their punters. In the jeweller's window hung a small black sign which read, in gold Gothic letters: A BACHELOR FIRST HAS HIS FLING, THEN ENDS UP GREY-HAIRED AND DEJECTED. MAX BUSSE HAS A GOLDEN RING, FOR ALL THE MEN WHO AREN'T REJECTED. Perhaps that did the trick?

Until a short while before, at the far end of the Rochstrasse, beyond the crossroads, Jewish bakers from Poland used to sell onion tarts with poppy seeds: round, flat, crusty pastries made with goose fat. The whole street smelled so wonderful that it made your mouth water. Now the shops stood empty. Where had all the bakers gone?

Uncle Meier went out only once a day, in the afternoon, to take the air. The black homburg hat and the velvet collar on his navy-blue cashmere coat would be brushed down. Aunt had neatly hand-stitched his yellow star on to his sleeve. Before he went out he sprinkled a little Uralt Lavendel on his hands and rubbed it into his face. Then he took up his silver-topped, bamboo walking stick and strolled to the Alexanderplatz and back.

Every year when the lavender is in bloom I only have to crush a sprig between my fingers and for a moment the scent brings Uncle Meier back to life again.

Uncle came home laughing: 'Today I helped a young woman to bring up her child. She kept calling out, "Come here, will you", but the boy pretended not to hear. Then she hissed at him: "Come here at once! And watch out, there's a Jew behind you. He's coming to get you." The boy ran to his mother as though the devil was after him.' My uncle grinned: 'Do you think the mother even thanked me?'

Next door to the entrance of No. 11 Münzstrasse was a toy shop specializing in model railways. The individual carriages were about the size of army loaves. These were toys for grown-ups with big wallets. They said this was where Reich Marshal Goering bought the carriages for the train set he kept in the cellar at Karinhall, his country estate. It amazed me that Hermann Goering ever found his way to No. 11 Münzstrasse.

Although the house stood in a rather run-down area, it was one of the more imposing buildings in the neighbourhood. The entrance hall boasted a mosaic floor, from which a huge spiral staircase took off, to wind its way from one storey to the next. There were three apartments on each floor. On the landing of the fifth floor, where we lived, my cousin and I used to lean over the banister playing 'who can dangle his spit longest' (you were allowed to suck it up again now and then). The winner was the one whose spit was the last to land with a splash on the stone floor below.

Next door to us lived old Frau Schumacher with her daughter and her grandson Horst. Once, when Mama had just come back from Frau Schumacher's place, she asked me: 'Have you noticed that Horst's Mama hasn't been around for some time, Cioma? Now I know why. She's doing three months in prison. Downstairs, on the wall of the house, someone had written in a childish hand: "All Hitlers are murderers." The Gestapo told the young woman outright that it was her boy who had done it. Frau Eberhard probably denounced her. She was the one with her arm in splints – she just *had* to see the Führer over the cheering crowds, so she climbed on a wall and fell off. What is it Wilhelm Busch said: "If someone who has only just managed to climb a tree starts thinking he's a bird, he's making a mistake."'

After the bomb fell on us, all three households were

lodged at No. 11 Münzstrasse: Uncle Meier, Aunt Soschka, Grandma, Mama and me. The rooms were crammed full of furniture, crockery, cutlery and bed linen. It looked like a warehouse, but even so it was very tidy and orderly.

Although it was practically impossible to emigrate by then,[15] the Jewish community was still allowed to offer English lessons. The light of the desk lamp Dorothee had given me as a present before she left shone down on the exercise book with my English homework in it. I needed to study hard, because I wanted to get into the evening classes for advanced students. I wasn't particularly good at English in school, but there was a girl on the advanced course who was worth any amount of effort.

I aimed to get on to the same course as her, and perhaps even sit next to her. The trouble was that another boy was already sitting there. His face was covered in acne. But his English was better than the teacher's. Why was he on the course? Because of Eva Goldschmidt? But why did Eva idolize him? I couldn't understand it. Did she already have some premonition that Gerhard Löwenthal was to become a famous TV journalist in the 1960s? I took some trouble over her all the same, and managed to strike up a conversation. What about? About Sigmund Freud and psychoanalysis. Would I lend her a book about it? 'Yes, why not.'

I invited her to come out in a rowing boat with me. It made me terrifically proud to see all the boys turning around to look at her. We bought a balloon at a fairground, and launched it with my address attached. One day I got a postcard: 'Today one of my pupils found the balloon with your address in a field. This little balloon managed to fly almost a hundred kilometres. What an amazing achievement for a toy airship. Heil Hitler, Senior Teacher Hartmut Hildebrand.'

Eva sat with me on a bench in the Tiergarten. I put my arm

around her, and then she confessed to me: 'You know, our friendship has no future. I've just got my visa for Portugal and they're letting me emigrate to join my aunt there. And anyway, you're much too young for me.' She was fifteen! 'And I'm afraid I can't give the Sigmund Freud back to you. My mother took it away. She said that young girls had no business reading Sigmund Freud, and my mother is a nurse. If you want it back you'll have to come round and get it yourself.'

I saw her home, and asked for my book back. Her mother, a little taller than me, gave me a dressing down: 'So, young man, let me tell you something: when you're talking to me, you take your hands out of your pockets, please, and the sweet out of your mouth. Then you can have your Freud back.' She began to laugh: 'But joking aside, drop in some time. Psychoanalysis is an interesting topic of conversation.'

Paul Levi, Karl Wiesner and I stuck loyally together. The hot steam irons at the workshop could not dampen our spirits. But Walter Prager could: 'Schönhaus, I've got to throw you out. It's a shame: but I want you to survive. And that's why you've got to move to the armaments industry. Here at Wysocky's I can't stop you from being "evacuated".' 'But, Herr Prager, you've got such good connections in high places.' He sat down near the ironing table and spoke so low that the others could not hear. 'Yes, and it's precisely because of my good connections that I know. You'll only be safe in a branch of the armaments industry where they do metalwork. I'll try to place you with Gustav Genschow in Treptow. It's a factory where they make small-bore arms. That's all I can do for you now.'

At the Labour Exchange, the man at the counter put two pieces of paper in my hand. One of them, as well as giving the address of Genschow's firm, read: 'Working hours six till six. One week day shift, one week night shift.' With this came a corresponding permit to use public transport.[16] I felt as though I was on the barrack square already: 'Fall in at six in the mornin'! Got that?'

On my very first day I arrived late. At the gate the helmeted soldier with his sloped rifle took no notice of me. I raced up the stairs. Suddenly Dr Selbiger stood in front of me, a teacher from my former school. 'So, Schönhaus. It's always the same ones who come late!' Like all the workers there, he wore oil-stained blue overalls. And a yellow star on the left side of his chest. But his face, with its black moustache twirled upwards and its bushy eyebrows behind the rimless spectacles, still inspired respect in me. (At school we called him a 'rotten swine' behind his back because he used to administer cuffs on the ear that left their mark for a long time afterwards.)

Now he remarked in a collegial manner: 'Arriving late is not quite so harmless here as it was at school, Schönhaus. There's a sign on the second floor that says if you arrive late three times you've got to report to Herr Rensing. On his door it says, ON STATE SECRET POLICE [Gestapo] SERVICE. So if you're late twice more you're in trouble. Give me your clocking-in card. I'll show you how to stamp it. Look, today your time is printed in red. If you get here punctually you'll have a blue stamp.'

The waiting room without hope

There was no box to catch the letters behind the door of our apartment. When the post came, I heard the footsteps of the postman approaching, and then the envelope plopped straight on to the polished parquet floor of the corridor.

The letter had no stamp, just a postmark. So I knew it must be from the police. My aunt appeared, clutching her dressing gown around her: 'Who is the letter from?' 'Mother and I have been summoned. We've got to present ourselves to the Gestapo at nine o'clock on Tuesday. In Burgstrasse, Room 23.' Uncle stood behind her, his damp hair constrained by a hairnet. My aunt breathed a sigh of relief: 'Not us, then.' 'Why isn't Cioma at work?' asked Uncle. 'You know why. He's got a certificate from his employer. And now just calm down. Take some valerian and go back to bed. The summons is not for us.'

Armed with the letter from the armaments factory I went with Mama on the Tuesday to Burgstrasse. We made for Room 23.

The Gestapo building used to be the stock exchange office block. From the outside, nothing much had changed. The quarry-stone exterior just looked a bit redder, almost as though it had absorbed the blood of the people processed there.

The gateway looked like the door of a big safe. An SS guard stood in front of it, his rifle shouldered. Mama showed him the summons. The gate opened quite slowly, as though of its own accord. We were free to go in.

Inside, there was a heavy iron grill, closed. In front of it there was a counter. We had to fill in a form. (As though they did not know who they had summoned.) So: surname, first name, date of birth etc. At the end came the information that the person concerned was only allowed to leave the premises with the permission of the official who had conducted the interrogation. With a signature, naturally. Whether we would be home again by that evening depended on this signature. On the wall hung a yellow cardboard direction sign: WAITING ROOM FOR JEWS, SECOND FLOOR, ON THE LEFT AT END OF CORRIDOR.

The gate shut behind us. We mounted a stone staircase to the second floor, and passed Room 23 on our way to the waiting room for Jews. It was a dead end. Surely no official would ever come to collect us from there. 'Yes, they will,' thought Mama. 'They've got to come for us.' 'Mama, I'm going to scout forward and have a look. Otherwise we'll still be sitting here tomorrow.' 'Don't do anything you shouldn't, Cioma. Isn't it enough that Papa's stuck in prison?' 'Don't worry. I'll call you when the door of Room 23 opens.'

The official was wearing a knitted waistcoat. He looked like a respectable middle-class family man, half-moon spectacles perched on the tip of his nose. 'Sit down, Frau Schönhaus.' He looked at us over his glasses. 'And there's a chair for your son. Frau Schönhaus, you know all Jews are now being evacuated to the east. For labour service. Actually you should have gone long ago. But, as I have established, your husband is still serving a prison sentence. The fact is that we at the Gestapo do not like separating family members. That is why I arranged for your leaving date to be postponed. In the meantime, I shall be asking for a pardon for your husband. Then you can all travel together. I have just seen that your son is in a reserved occupation in the arms industry, at Gustav Genschow's. But I will intervene there as well and ensure that he does not have to stay behind in Berlin by himself. Be ready to report at the former synagogue in Levetzowstrasse some time during the next three weeks. That's the collecting point for the transports leaving from Grunewald station for the Generalgouvernement, that is to say what used to be Poland. I'll sign your permit so that you'll have no trouble getting out. All the best then, Frau Schönhaus.'

Mama stroked my hair. 'Many thanks, Herr Kommissar.' And we went down the stone steps. 'Actually, he was quite decent,' my mother said. Hardly had she finished speaking when an SS officer in his smart uniform came up the stairs

towards us, pushing a prisoner in front of him. His stinking prison clothes flapped around his skinny limbs. As the prisoner struggled up laboriously, one step at a time, the SS officer struck him a blow in the back of the neck. The prisoner collapsed, but was just able to catch himself up in time. The SS man shouted: 'If you give out on me now, you know what to expect!'

Mother went as white as a sheet. She clutched at her throat as though she were going to be sick. I took her hand. She held mine tight until we reached the street. She looked at me with tears in her eyes. 'Cioma, what sort of person is that? Hasn't he got any feelings at all? How can anyone be so vicious? Hasn't that monster got a soul in his body? Can't he understand other people's feelings? What kind of a world is it where such creatures can rule Germany?'

The weather outside was brilliant. 'They can do everything else, Cioma, but they can't stop the sun shining.' We put our arms round each other. Mama went off to Wysocky's workshop, and I took the S-Bahn overland train to Gustav Genschow's factory at Treptow.

At the lathe

The train doors closed automatically. The train was practically empty. A man with a shock of white hair was standing in a connecting corridor, holding his hat so that his face was half hidden. He looked at me, turning round to check whether anyone was watching him. Then he turned back to me and pointed to his coat, indicating my star. Then he looked at me with a barely perceptible shake of his head. He got out at Rummelsburg station, but turned round twice more on the platform to see if he was being followed. Nobody had been watching him. Only me.

Then the compartment began to fill up. A group of workers got on. A fat man took a window seat. Another man wanted to sit next to him: 'Move over, you black marketeer.' 'What do you mean, black marketeer?' he replied angrily. 'Well, you can't get as fat as that on the rations they give us.' Everybody laughed.

Treptow station. I got out. Treptow Park with its massive trees was a green oasis in the midst of the metropolis. It was criss-crossed by narrow paths. In the summer the ice-cream vendors stood there selling ices from their carts: coffee, vanilla and strawberry. It was still cold, though, and anyway there was a war on. I was just about to cross the road, when a marching column came towards me. Strangely silent. At closer range I could see why: they were all barefoot. They were

Russian women – forced labour. On their jackets you could see the blue cloth labels with white lettering: EAST.

The Gustav Genschow factory had been sprayed with fire hoses in green, brown and black camouflage paint, as protection from enemy bombers. An armed sentry in matching tones stood at the gate. I showed my ID card and he waved me on. The black and white tile steps to the factory hall were sprinkled with sawdust to prevent people from slipping. The hall, on the second floor, contained lathes, standing on wooden flooring which absorbed the noise of the machines but was saturated with crude oil. The air, too, was misty with the oil emulsion that cooled down the glowing steel swarf spiralling off from each component as it was machined. The shavings glowed prettily, purple, red and yellow, until they dropped into the waste bin.

I stood at the lathe allocated to me while the Aryan overseer explained my job. The master, or foreman, Ackermann, came past. He had a nose like a hawk, but Ackermann was no bird of prey. He was all laughter, from head to foot. He had to force himself to be serious. 'So, the lads at the Gestapo have let you go again? Was my certificate any good to you?' Although I hadn't actually used it, I said 'yes'. He winked at me, and then he was off to the next lathe. I asked the overseer: 'What do they actually produce here?' 'Heck, the questions you ask. We're bringing shooting up to date! We turn old rifle barrels into sub-machine gun barrels. They're extremely handy, and you can fire much faster with them.'

I wondered whether I might be shot one day with a handy sub-machine gun. And again I heard Papa: 'Don't think about it . . . don't think about it . . .'

'Don't think about what might happen tomorrow. Do what you can today. You'll be doing it for yourself. Learn another profession. Show how well we Jews can work. Make hard soap. Do what is possible today. Let the Lord take care of tomorrow.' Papa's voice was so loud in my head that I looked round to see whether he was actually standing next to me. And although I knew they might come for me at any time, suddenly I was enjoying the work. I couldn't help thinking all the while that one day they might shoot me with a barrel I had made on my own lathe, but all the same . . .

I would not let the overseer machine the steel for me: I wanted to do it myself. 'I'll make an exception,' he said. I learnt how to adjust the lathe down to the last hundredth of a millimetre. Laughing, the overseer said: 'Now you don't need me any more at all.' Gradually the setting of the lathe became so precise that it automatically reduced the gun barrels to the prescribed measurement. The lathe was humming. Everything was working automatically. All I had to do was clamp the work in, turn the crank, take out the barrel, check the measurements, fit another barrel . . . Clamp, turn, remove and fit . . .

I spent this time daydreaming, staring out of the huge factory window. It was worth it. Outside there was a large market garden with blue-green cabbages. Van Gogh could not have painted them better. In the distance I could see Berlin through the haze of smoke from the factory chimneys. Standing at the lathe, I painted this picture again and again in my mind. After the war I would come back and set up my easel here. That was it: I would be a painter. While I was daydreaming, I noticed two gentlemen observing me. One of them was holding a stopwatch. 'Good, just carry on, Schönhaus.' 'He's really got the whole thing down to a fine art. He even has time to keep taking a rest in between. And he machines the steel himself, too.' 'Fantastic.'

Next day my work was interrupted. Another lathe was being set up next to mine. Instead of staring out of the window daydreaming, I now had to work two machines at a time. I still thought I could manage the work in my sleep, and went on abandoning myself to my daydreams.

Actually I was supposed to check the length after every tenth barrel. But in my dreamy state I forgot to do so until a hundred had gone through. Whoops! They were all too short! Rejects. 'Sabotage!' ran through my head. My heart was pounding. What to do? At such moments I always looked deep inside myself to seek advice: 'Cioma, what you've got to do is make out that things are much worse than they are. The damage you've done must appear trivial compared with what you have prepared the boss for.'

As luck would have it, the foreman that day was Herr Schwarz, the top master craftsman in the machine room. Particularly worrying was the small SS button he wore in his lapel. And he was the one I now had to confess to. 'Boss, I've done something really, really terrible.' 'Why? What have you done? Wrecked your lathe? Or what?' 'No, not that. But I've shortened a hundred barrels by seven hundredths too much.' 'Ruddy hell, you gave me a terrible shock. Chuck the barrels in the reject bin, lad. The loss will be taken off your wages.'

In the 1930s the Schönhaus mineral water plant still used to deliver its products by horse and cart. We had seven horses and three draymen. Herbert Richard was one of them. Unfortunately, he couldn't drive a van. So Papa eventually had to ask him to go. But he still came round to see us now and again, particularly then, when my mother was having such a tough time. His wife offered to take in my mother's washing for her, and that was an advantage for me, because unlike my Jewish workmates, who arrived in the mornings with their clothes still oily, thanks to Frau Richard I always turned up in clean clothes.

Perhaps that was why Director Wagner came and stood behind me one afternoon, and tapped me on the shoulder.

'Schönhaus, would you like to learn to use a file? Then you can have a new job, like the Aryan workers. You'll be trained, and you'll even be able to sit on a stool while you work.'

Naturally I accepted. Like all apprentice metalworkers, I began by learning how to file a cube. A cube must have the same measurements on all six sides. I got the hang of it pretty quickly, and then I moved on to the real work. The barrel of a machine gun rested in a u-shaped channel. With the recoil of every round fired, the barrel travelled to and fro, guided by grooves milled out at the sides. These grooves, known as rails or guides, had to be filed down to the last hundredth of a millimetre, to prevent any side-play in the movement of the barrel. The sides were checked by measuring them with a calliper gauge, which acted like a kind of internal clamp. There was a tolerance of minus one hundredth of a millimetre at the front, and plus one hundredth at the rear. The callipers had to be able to wedge into and hang from the groove at the breech end, at the point where the second hundredth began. Then it was all right. If too much was filed off, the machine-gun part was only fit for scrap. So you had to watch out. There were officers sitting nearby in the workshop checking every part with their own gauges.

Another parting gift from Dorothee was a gramophone record: Tchaikovsky's *1812 Overture* on one side, Chopin's *Funeral March* on the other. The rhythms in the *Funeral March* pounded in your soul like hammer blows, as the dead man was accompanied on his last journey.

Mama cried whenever I played Chopin's *Funeral March*: 'Cioma, why are you playing that? Life is hard enough as it is. Must you make it harder? Turn it off, please. I can't stand that music.' 'OK, Mama, we'll turn the record over. You can hear how Napoleon was beaten in Russia in 1812.'

At first the Russians retreat. But during the night, in their forests, they plan a surprise attack on the French. A French scout is captured, and he is forced to listen while they play their balalaikas, and watch them dancing the Krakoviak. He feels his hours are numbered. Then a new day dawns. A rider on a prancing white horse reconnoitres the valley. He bears a tricolour. The roar of the *Marseillaise* advances. Thousands of French cuirassiers gallop in waves over the Russian positions. But, led by the apparently unresisting Marshal Kutuzov, the Russian Army rises up. Distant bells toll out from the onion domes, as the two armies clash in battle. And amidst the pealing bells the Russian national anthem combats the *Marseillaise*, until gradually 'God save the Tsar' prevails and drowns out the fanfares of the invaders. With their last ounce of strength the Cossacks overwhelm all the French attackers. God has broken the neck of the French. The solitary figure of Napoleon flees in his sleigh through an endless Russia towards his downfall.

The same would happen to Hitler. 'That's how it will be, Mama; God will save us too.' 'Yes, Ciomka. He'll save you. You will survive. You will tell people about us. But I'm going with Papa to Poland or God knows where. I'll never leave him. But you, my child, must live and be healthy. And play the defeat of Napoleon rather than Chopin's *Funeral March*.'

The compulsory oath of disclosure

About a hundred people were waiting in the street. Many knew each other. They stood there as though queuing at a theatre box office. But it was not a box office. It was a side entrance to the hall of the Jewish congregation in the synagogue building in the Oranienburger Strasse. The huge dome with its gilded ribs still gleamed in the sunlight, but now the building was a branch of the Gestapo.

All the people standing there had to sign – voluntarily, of course – that they relinquished all their property in favour of the German Reich.[17] We had nothing left. No money, no houses, no land, no cars. Not even a cat or a dog. Many of those standing there had been quite well off that morning; now they were beggared. Dispossessed. Outlawed. They all signed. Officials of the Jewish community had to collect the signatures and check them off. There was no sign of the Gestapo. Now we were the equals of the affluent. It was so easy to possess nothing. This was how birds must feel as they fly freely across the sky over all the frontiers.

Mama said goodbye to a woman I did not know. We went back to Münzstrasse. It wasn't far, but we were dead tired. I was looking forward to bed, because I was on night shift and had to get my sleep.

There was a man standing in the street outside our house. He must once have been very fat. His trousers were hanging around him like a sack. His double chin reached almost to his shoulders. But it was empty now. Too much skin. His watery eyes blinked beneath his seaman's cap as he saw us coming. 'So, there you are. I thought you had already been sent away. I've brought you something to eat. Can I come in?' 'But Herr Lehmann, aren't you afraid?' 'God no, no one's going to do anything to me. I know how to defend myself against these villains.' He emptied his rucksack. 'Right, here's smoked sausage, Edam cheese, and half a pound of butter. I got it all from an old supplier to my restaurant.'

'Herr Lehmann was one of our first customers, Cioma, when Papa still had his mineral water company.' 'Yes, Herr Schönhaus. I taught your father how to sling a thirty-bottle case of mineral water on to his back without losing a single bottle. And your Mama was very pleased when I tried to persuade him that a mineral water producer shouldn't wear a torn jacket. But your father said he didn't care.'

'Herr Lehmann, can I ask you a question? I don't want to go to Poland. But if I stay here I'll have to go into hiding. Can you help me?' 'Well, there would always be some warm soup at our place for you, of course. But staying with us is a tricky business. My wife is very nervous, and she's got a heart condition, too. But yes, if it comes to it, we'll sort something out.'

He glanced around, as though looking for something. Then his gaze fixed on the large dining-room lamp. 'It's a real shame about this lovely lamp.' Mama shook her head. 'But we can't sit here in the dark until they come for us, Herr Lehmann.' 'Oh well, Frau Schönhaus. It was just a thought.'

Herr Lehmann had left. Now I had to get to sleep quickly, because even by one minute past six the clocking-in machine stamped your card red.

In the old days Papa used to beat out the rhythm of a moving train on my bedcover. But now, when I listened carefully, it was the hoof beats of a galloping horse I could hear. I was galloping with loose reins in 3/4 time through the winter's night. I swayed gently in the saddle and asked Papa: 'Where is the stallion taking me?' And from a distance there came: 'Don't think about it . . . don't think about it . . . don't think about it . . .' The horse's hooves crunched through the snow. It wasn't difficult to catch up with the troika in which Napoleon was fleeing to Paris. I shouted to the Emperor: 'Too late, Bonaparte. You've lost!' But then my steed unexpectedly stopped. Suddenly there was a wall in front of us, blocking the way. And hanging on the wall was a picture of Napoleon; his right hand was tucked into his waistcoat, the left behind his back. That's the way everybody knows him. The Emperor asked his picture: 'What's going to happen, Bonaparte?' and the picture answered: 'Nothing is going to happen. Everything is going to stay as it is. Except that you and I will change places. I will be taken down and you will be hung up.' Then Napoleon drew out his pistol. His sleigh was getting closer. My steed began to trot. There was a shot. It didn't hit me, but my stallion turned into a racehorse. The foam from his mouth was hitting my face. I had to sit lightly, or I would have been thrown from the saddle. No good trying to rein him in. Instead, I spurred him on, so that at least I could control his direction. I managed to veer left at the next fork in the road. That was just as well, because the signpost there pointed to Switzerland. But I had not yet reached the border. My stallion stumbled over a bell wire. 'Aha,' I thought, 'that's the border. I had better cross it on foot, because my horse hasn't got any papers.' But the bell wire didn't stop ringing; it rang and rang and rang. Until in the end I opened my eyes. It was my alarm clock, which I had stood on two soup plates, combined to form a sounding board, so that I wouldn't oversleep.

Night shift from six till six

The 'Aryan' overseer kept a sharp eye on me while I was working with the file. He looked exactly the type to be recruited for Hitler's bodyguard, the 'Leibstandarte Adolf Hitler',[18] except that at sixty plus he was now too old. He made me nervous. Every time I checked with the gauge, I found I had filed off too much. I threw channel iron after channel iron into the waste bin. It sounded like breaking glass.

My 'Aryan' boss bent down close to my ear. 'Lad, you're creating too much waste. It doesn't take them long around here to start talking about sabotage. It's better to give it a knock on the head.' 'How do you mean?' 'With the hammer. At night, when we're more or less alone, and nobody's watching!' 'I don't understand.' 'OK, listen. When you've filed off too much, take the hammer and hit the end of the channel. You'll compress the metal and cause a burr. And when the officers come to check the measurement, their calliper gauge gets caught on the burr so that it hangs from it, and everything is in order. The machine-gun barrel will only start to waver when it's used in combat. And if our soldiers miss, and somebody they're trying to shoot stays alive by mistake, that's fine by us, OK? Are we agreed? But keep your mouth shut, lad, otherwise we're both for it!' And I had been sure that somebody so 'Aryan'-looking must be a Nazi. How wrong you can be. Now at last my work had a purpose. And I had a friend on the night shift.

On the corner of Grenadierstrasse and Linienstrasse, two young men were fighting. One was a soldier, the other still a civilian. Chin-hooks and side-swipes were flying about. People were standing around. Me too. The civilian got the upper hand. The soldier finished up lying in a puddle. But then he shouted in a thin, cracked, high-pitched voice: 'Just you wait, you swine. You'll pay for this. You've insulted my uniform. You have insulted a German uniform!' 'Hell, Paule, I didn't mean to. Come on, let's bury the hatchet.' The soldier got up from the pavement. They shook hands.

I took a parcel of dirty laundry to Frau Richard in Grenadierstrasse. The street, formerly the centre of the Jewish area, the Scheunenviertel, now seemed dead. Only the faded lettering in Hebrew script spelling 'kosher' recalled the Jewish life that had departed.

The windows of the former Hassidic[19] prayer rooms were blind. They looked inwards. They were dreaming. The faint reflections of the joyful Hassidim could still be seen in the dull windows, dancing in their fur-trimmed hats, their long coats and their unpolished peasant boots. They circled ecstatically, clapping their hands and singing God's praises. Once ashamed of Jewish waywardness, contrasting so much with the clean straight lines of the marching columns, now I was suddenly full of yearning for lost, warm, colourful Jewish life. 'Creating order' is the Germans' magic invocation.

I went into No. 12, where Herbert Richard lived, to collect my clean laundry and leave the dirty stuff. In the entrance to the building I had a terrible shock: the ceiling of the entrance hall was specked with human ordure, little brown sausages stuck everywhere; the smell was bestial. I held my nose and rang the doorbell. The nameplate said HERBERT RICHARD, HAULAGE CONTRACTOR. 'Herr Richard, what on earth has been going on here?' 'The landlord lives on this floor, Herr Schönhaus. He had a row with a neighbour, and yesterday the neighbour came and rang the landlord's bell, and the second he opened the door, he threw a full chamber pot in his face. This ceiling thing only happened because the landlord got so worked up trying to get his revenge.' I took my clean washing, paid, thanked him, and went back to No. 11 Münzstrasse.

At home there was a man sitting at our kitchen table. He was pale and unshaven, but he looked peaceful and relaxed. Mama introduced him to me: 'Cioma, this is Herr Schlesinger. He was in prison with Papa. He was released this morning. But Herr Schlesinger, why don't you tell my son what you've just told me.'

'Yes, I've brought good wishes from your father. He is my best friend. I've never respected anyone as much as him. Everyone likes him, even the prison officer. You know the story of the soap? That's just typical. The things he finds in the rubbish are incredible. He's the only one who's got any nail scissors. But you should have seen what they looked like when he picked them up. Now they're clean and sharp and you can use them. And nobody knows the value of nail scissors in prison unless they've been inside themselves. He renovates old razor blades. One of his favourite sayings is "A good shave makes a good mood."' 'Yes,' said my mother, 'he even said that in one of his recent letters to me. It's not exactly philosophy, but I'm glad to know he's cheerful.'

'You know, Frau Schönhaus, what I admire most about him is his self-discipline. Let me tell you a story about the daily bread ration. Prison bread is damp, sticky stuff, but everybody waits ravenously for it, all the same. Your husband is the only one strong-willed enough to save some of his ration, to build up a spare piece that has had time to dry out a bit. But hang on, I haven't told you the most important part yet. When a Jewish prisoner is released he doesn't get any food during the last twenty-four hours of his stay in gaol. Everybody knows that. That was why your husband gave me his spare piece of bread as a leaving present. But when I went to eat his bread on my last day, somebody had stolen it. And what did Boris Schönhaus do? He gave me his other piece, and went without for twenty-four hours instead of me. You can be proud of him. And you might ask why they let a Jew like me out. I don't know. Because normally Jews who have served prison sentences get sent straight off to concentration camp or are evacuated to Poland. But maybe Heaven kept me back so that I could come and tell you about your father. Now I'm going to try to go underground in Berlin. Officially I still live here, with my wife, for the time being. Here's my address: Ruth and Werner Schlesinger, 24 Ansbacher Strasse, Berlin.'

'I'm going to stay in Berlin in hiding, too, Herr Schlesinger,' I said.

'Perhaps we can help each other.'

'Date of deportation: 2 June 1942'

Mama was heating the stove for a bath. First you had to put in newspaper and kindling. Then you put on briquettes, and at the end a piece of firelighter, to help the burning match make the fire catch light. While the hot bath water was running, Mama sang an old Russian folksong: '*Prashchaitye gory i lesa,yia uyezhayu na vsegda.*' (Farewell you mountains and forests, I am leaving for ever.)

The next day was 2 June 1942, the day for us to report at Levetzowstrasse. There was no knowing when I might get another bath. The cyclostyled list of all the things you had to take with you was quite reassuring. Would you need all this on a journey to your death?

2 pairs of waterproof shoes
4 pairs of socks
6 pairs of underpants
2 pullovers
2 blankets
4 shirts
1 hat or cap
2 pairs of gloves
1 overcoat
1 rucksack

Mama's rucksack was full to bursting. I didn't have one, because I wasn't going. Or so I hoped.

It was only the day before, at work, that foreman Schwarz had given me the letter of appeal for exemption, although I had asked for it a fortnight earlier:

Gustav Genschow, Small Arms Manufacturer, Berlin Treptow, 31 May 1942

This is to certify that Cioma Israel Schönhaus is employed in our firm as a precision engineer. He is an important worker. We request an extension of exemption for him. Heil Hitler. Signed: Schwarz, Foreman and SS Captain.

It was too late to send the letter by post. 'Come on, Cioma, we'll go to the Gestapo in Burgstrasse this evening and hand the letter in there.'

The SS sentry at the gate would not let us in. 'Too late,' he said, 'Give me the letter. I'll pass it on.' 'But we're due to be transported in the morning.' 'So what? It's not as though you'll have left this world behind by tomorrow.'

Mama put her arm through mine. We went home together. Each of us sunk in thought. Our ways might part the next day. Who could tell?

The next day came. I was utterly determined to act as though I had already been exempted; as though the Gustav Genschow request had already been granted; as though I didn't have to go with the transport at all. I left as usual to get to work by six o'clock. I said goodbye to Mama when I set off, as if I would be seeing her again that evening. Except that, contrary to our usual habits, we gave each other a hug before I went.

At the factory I clocked in as usual. Everything was normal. Except that I couldn't take a deep breath, because of the choking in my throat. While I was clamping a u-channel into my vice as usual, a workman came by and whispered: 'The *chasarim* (pigs) are here, Schönhaus.' Two quite ordinary-looking men in civilian clothes were standing there. They kept their hats on while they were talking to foreman Schwarz.

Then they showed him a document. He brought them over to me: 'Schönhaus! Get changed. You're coming with us.' I collected my jacket from the cloakroom. Then the three of us walked through Treptow Park, not to the S-Bahn but to the tram stop.

To all appearances everything was quite normal. The two men calmly discussed their schedule. There was someone else to be picked up at the Spittelmarkt. We went up to the second floor there, just as though I was one of them. A Star of David had been stuck to the wall next to a nameplate saying LEVI. One of the men rang the bell. Nothing happened. He tried again. Nobody opened. 'Come on, let's go. We'll pick him up later.' We went back to the tram.

We stood on the platform at the rear. I looked at the two of them. What sort of people were these? One looked as though he might have been a bookkeeper in a bank. Somebody who had the job of working through the accounts beginning with 'J'. The other one might have been a print compositor who had to give up his job because of an allergy to lead type. The bookkeeper's face was the more humane-looking of the two. I spoke to him: 'Look, I didn't expect to be deported. I haven't even got a warm coat with me. Couldn't we collect it from my place? The tram goes right past the flat.' He turned to his colleague: 'What do you think?' 'It's all the same to me. Why shouldn't he fetch his overcoat?'

My aunt opened the door and looked at us wide-eyed. She said not a word, but her face was full of fear. While I got my coat from the wardrobe, the typesetter sat down at my desk as if it were his own. He rummaged in the drawer, found a box containing my father's gold wedding ring, and tucked the ring away in his waistcoat pocket just as though he'd left it somewhere and finally found it again.

It was warm on the tram. We stood on the rear platform

once more. My overcoat was hanging over my arm. 'But young man, you haven't got a star on it,' said the bookkeeper. 'Without a star they'll take it off you again straight away.' 'Well, I've got a spare star in my pocket, but I can't sew it on: I haven't got a needle and thread.' 'Hold on a second. Let's see what we can do.' He produced a little packet of needles and thread from his wallet. 'Mind you, you'll have to do the sewing yourself.'

While I was sewing, stitch by stitch, a woman got on. Almond-eyed, petite, with a huge rucksack on her back, and a yellow star in front, on the left. Hardly had she stepped on board when a soldier jumped up and offered her his seat. Now the bookkeeper showed a different face. He went up to the soldier: 'How dare you, a German soldier, sully the honour of your uniform? How can you be so shameless as to publicly offer your seat to a Jewish woman? You're going to pay dearly for this, my friend. What? Answering back as well? You could see perfectly well she's a Jewess. The star looks big enough to me. Name? Number? Regiment? Where are you stationed? And don't make it worse by getting impudent with me!' He came back to me snorting. I returned his sewing kit. 'Many thanks.' 'You're welcome.' He put the packet back in his wallet. 'There's got to be order!' The conductor shouted: 'Levetzowstrasse!' 'Right, here's where we get off.'

A lot of benches were arranged across the hall of the former synagogue in Levetzowstrasse. About six hundred people sat there waiting, some young, but most of them elderly. The majority were warmly dressed. Rather too warmly for the time of year. Many sat silent; others were talking, gesticulating from time to time, as though in a railway station waiting room. Except that nobody knew when the train was due to leave, or its destination. However, they were all encouraged a little by the sight of young Jewish girls in snow-white aprons handing out tasty macaroni garnished with cheese. The dishes were much bigger than the appetites of those forced to wait there.

I looked everywhere for my mother. In the end I found her in a corner of the hall, talking to a woman we knew, a neighbour. Her face lit up when she saw me. She smiled: 'I knew this morning that we'd see each other again soon. Now we can stay together, and it won't be as bad as you think. Look over there. There's been an official examining our luggage ever since I arrived. And by the way, where is your luggage?' 'I couldn't bring anything but my overcoat.' 'Well, that's something, anyway. It can be very cold in Poland or Russia.' She put her arm round my shoulder and looked down one of the corridors. 'I think Papa will be coming from that direction.'

In the middle of the synagogue, on the dais where they used to read from the Torah during services, there was a typewriter, with a Jewish steward sitting in front of it, flanked by a Gestapo officer. Another Jewish steward was leaning over the balustrade, standing on tiptoe, holding on tight and screaming out at the top of his lungs the names of people due to be deported to the east next morning.

No doubt his predecessor had failed to shout loud enough and had been packed off without warning on the next transport. This steward wanted to avoid the same fate; like the cockerel in the Town Band of Bremen, crowing as loudly as he could to stay out of the cooking pot: 'Hans Israel Rosenzweig ... Hans Israel Rosenzweig ... Hans Israel Rosenzweig ...'

The names proceeded alphabetically: Schönhaus would soon follow. Mama and I sat close to each other. I told her about the Kaiserhof and the bar where I had drunk whisky with Det and the two sailors, and about the policeman I had sent to arrest his drunken colleague who accused every customer in the café of being a Jew. 'But, Cioma, how could you do such dangerous things? Just as well I didn't know about it at the time.' I took her hand. In her blue suit with the white blouse she was my sister, my friend, my mother.

Strange how loud it sounded when your own name was bellowed out across the hall. The names that had already been read out had faded into the crowd. But when you heard 'Samson Cioma Israel Schönhaus and Fanja Sara Schönhaus', your heart shrank. Our legs were set in motion as though by an unseen force, and we were standing on the dais. Mama squeezed my hand. As cool as ice, the Jewish steward read out our files: 'Fanja Sara Schönhaus and her son, Samson Cioma Israel Schönhaus, are ordered to go with the transport for the east tomorrow morning, 2 June 1942. On behalf of the son there is a request from the firm of Gustav Genschow. He is a good worker and therefore indispensable. They request that his evacuation be deferred to a later date.'

While this was being read out, the uniformed Gestapo official was looking right through me with his watery blue eyes. He had turned his chair round and was leaning vacantly on the seat back. 'Should the young man go with the transport, or should he stay here?' the steward asked. 'OK, yeah,' the Gestapo man replied, too bored to open his mouth properly. It was as if he was counting off the decision on his buttons: 'Stay here – go – stay here – go – stay here – go – stay here. I don't care. OK, yeah. He's going.'

The steward repeated in a matter-of-fact tone: 'It has just been decided that you will go with the transport tomorrow!' All I could feel were my hot, sweating feet. The toes were sticking together. Confused thoughts ran through my head. If only I could change my socks. But I haven't got any other socks. I haven't got any socks at all. I've got no luggage. Only a briefcase with my sandwiches, and my overcoat. And I had

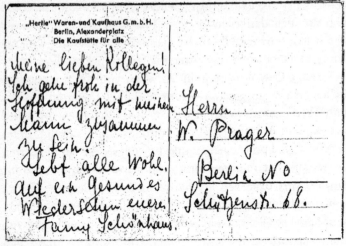

The card reads:
'*Dear workmates,*
I'm happy to set off in the hope of being together with my husband. Goodbye everybody;
I look forward to seeing you all again in good health.
Yours
Fanny Schönhaus'

My mother wrote this card in all confidence and innocence before her deportation to the
Majdanek death-camp.
I was supposed to add a stamp and post it, but forgot to do so. I was a bad son. Today this
card is precious to me.

been made to put that on top of a mountain of clothes. Would
I ever get it back?

Now Mama and I had to go down a wide corridor. On the
right were various doors to rooms with desks. An official sat
behind every desk. At every desk there was a white notice.
The first said FINANCE OFFICE. The official sat behind it as
though at a post-office counter: 'Have you got any money?'
'Yes, my lucky penny.' 'Right, hand it over.' And he entered on
a form: '1 penny.' No further mention of luck. At the second
desk the white sign said LABOUR OFFICE. Here a nice young
woman sat in front of a large filing cabinet. 'Where have you
been working?' 'At Gustav Genschow's.' Then I whispered:

'Actually, I'm exempt.' 'Just a moment,' she said, and started flicking through the file cards. 'Yes, here it is. Schönhaus. You're in a reserved occupation. One second!' She got up and went to see her supervisor.

At that moment, Papa suddenly emerged through a door on the left. He hugged first Mama, and then me. He stood there with his big moustache, in a grey gabardine coat. Now we were united. A little family, not to be parted. We waited.

People filed past the tables along the corridor handing over everything that might identify them, like living trees being stripped bare of leaves. We waited.

In the distance I could hear the young woman's animated tones. And then I heard her supervisor: 'But, my girl, if everybody who turns up here with a letter like this . . .' What followed was lost in the general hubbub of the waiting crowd. They've made a decision, I thought. And then she returned. With a smile: 'You can go.' 'Where to,' I asked. 'Home. You've been deferred.' Mama looked at Papa. 'What do you think? Should he stay behind?' 'Of course he should stay! Maybe he can rescue us.' I gave him my sandwiches. They had smoked Krakow sausage in them. I hugged my father and mother. 'Goodbye.' And we took our leave of each other. Not like on a station – no, it happened in a corridor in the former synagogue at Levetzowstrasse. For ever.

Like a sleepwalker I wandered past the great pile of clothes. My blue overcoat was still lying on the top. I put it over my arm. Nobody stopped me on the way out. The sentry at the door said nothing. I passed him and walked slowly down Levetzowstrasse. All I could feel were my burning feet. Nothing else. I halted at the next tram stop. The tram arrived. I got in. It had scarcely moved off when the conductor came up. He looked at me, glanced at the star on my coat, shook his head and asked: 'Have you got a travel permit for Jews? No?' He pulled the bell twice, and the tram came to a halt between stops. 'Please,' he said, pointing to the door, 'get off.' In the street it occurred to me that I didn't have the fare, anyway.

My reception by Uncle and Aunt was frosty. My bed had already been stripped. At last they had got rid of that awkward troublemaker. And now he was back again. He was constantly coming home after the official Jewish curfew hour. He was always running around without a star. He endangered everybody with his careless behaviour. All the same, I was given some soup, and had to tell them everything. Then I stood my alarm clock on the two soup plates and went to bed. Only Grandma came in, took my head between her hands, and pulled me towards her. I went to sleep, because the next morning I would be clocking in again at six at Gustav Genschow's.

After work I walked through Treptow Park to the S-Bahn station with a workmate, Walter Heyman, heading for home. Beech, ash and oak trees that must have seen the First World War stood out huge and dark against the night sky in blacked-out Berlin. The moon lit up our path. Walter Heyman had once been a journalist. He was a head shorter than me, his black hair combed sleekly back. It was glistening, not with brilliantine, but because of the oil-laden air in the machine room. A missing front tooth made him lisp. 'You know,' he said, 'Nietzsche once said that if something was falling, it should be pushed. We are being pushed.' 'But tell me, Herr Heyman, why have we Jews been persecuted ever since ancient times? It began with the Romans; or even earlier, with the Babylonians.' 'True, Schönhaus. And I'll tell you why. Do you know the parable of Abraham and his father? Abraham, the ancestor of all the Jewish people, was the son of a wood carver who made idols. One day, when Abraham was alone in the workshop, he took an axe and smashed all the idols to matchwood. He left only one figure intact, and under the arm of this idol he placed the axe.

"What's happened here?" shouted his father when he came back. "I don't know," replied Abraham. "The idols had an argument, and one of them slew all the others." "Are you trying to make a fool of me?" asked his father. "One idol can't have destroyed all the others with an axe." "You see," said Abraham, "that's why I don't believe in the power of these gods. There is only one God. And He is invisible. He reigns over us. And it is Him I believe in." To put it in a childishly simplified way, my dear Schönhaus, that was the beginning of our Jewish religion.'

There were a lot of benches in Treptow Park. On all of them it said in large yellow letters NOT FOR JEWS. 'Come on, Schönhaus, let's sit down.' Our briefcases came in handy not only for carrying sandwiches but also for hiding our yellow stars.

'But Herr Heyman, I'm still waiting for you to say why we Jews have been persecuted since time began.' 'My dear Schönhaus, the invisible Jewish God is superior to all the other, tangible gods. He makes everybody who believes in Him self-confident and superior. But self-confidence and superiority don't necessarily gain friends. That is one of the reasons why Jews have been persecuted. But not the only one. Our walk to the S-Bahn isn't long enough to mention them all. We'll talk again some other time.'

We were at the station. The train arrived and I had to get in. 'Yes, we'll come back to it next time.' Walter Heyman stayed on the platform. The doors closed automatically, operated by air pressure. And through the misted windows I saw him standing there, transformed: with a big moustache and wearing a grey gabardine coat. The train started.

The postcard

One morning just as I was on my way to the bathroom some post fell through the letter box. A postcard lay on the parquet floor of the corridor; postmark – Majdanek.[20] It was in Papa's neat writing, though written with a shaking hand: 'Dear people, I have arrived here safely. Have you heard anything from Fanja? I've been looking for Mama everywhere. Cioma was right about everything. I'm glad he's not here with us. Farewell, Your Beba.'

How had he managed to write this card without it being censored? Where did he get pen and ink? Where did he get the postcard? In Majdanek camp in Poland – a miracle. How did he pull it off? Typical of Papa. I held the card in my hand like a sacred relic. It was post from Beyond. I suppressed the volcano moving beneath my feet, on top of which I was trying to live as though there was no crater about to open and swallow me up.

The day at Gustav Genschow's started for me the same as ever with clocking in. Afterwards I sat on a high three-legged stool at my workbench. My Nordic-looking friend greeted me with a 'Good morning', winking at me imperceptibly with his left eye. Admittedly, I was no longer facing the big window looking out on the cabbage patch, the Van Gogh motif. To compensate, my workplace was now bathed in sunlight. And because I had stopped working at the lathe where your hands were constantly exposed to the flowing oil emulsion, I no longer had pimples on my forearms, unlike all my workmates who were still in the same job.

I was quietly whistling the 'Stephanie Gavotte' from a film I had seen recently. Meanwhile I was filing u-channels. The good ones in the pail, the bad ones in the bin. Suddenly an

Aryan worker behind me commented: 'Since when have Jews working here been allowed to sit?' I turned round. 'Mind your own bloody business.' He replied by clouting me in the face. My reflex reaction was to raise my hand to hit him back. With my hand barely lifted, the other man started bawling instantly. 'What? Daring to raise your hand against a German worker? That's going to cost you plenty!' 'I'm allowed to sit while filing. Director Wagner gave me explicit permission.'

Foreman Schwarz had heard our palaver. 'What's going on here?' All the workmen stood round us, the Jews a bit further away. The bully explained the situation: 'When I pointed out to him that Jews aren't allowed to sit at work, he gave me a cheeky answer. Then I hit him.' 'And what happened then?' asked the foreman. Nobody spoke. The bully didn't either. He said not a word about my raised hand. He didn't want to send me to concentration camp. Schwarz came to a decision: 'OK, Schönhaus will be docked this week's pay.'

During the break my Jewish colleagues congratulated me. 'You were lucky, Schönhaus. The worker who hit you was a leading member of the socialist trade union during the Weimar Republic.'

On our way home through Treptow Park, Walter Heyman quoted Erich Kästner: 'A slap like that in a cheerful face sounds pretty loud to the one on the receiving end. However, such slaps are not fatal. Man is built to withstand them.'

The big spiral staircase in Münzstrasse creaked once again under the postman's tread. And once more something fell through the letter box on to the parquet floor. This time there were two letters at once. One was a summons for Marie Sara Berman, née Romanov. My Grandma. It gave notice that she was to be taken to the retirement home of the Jewish Hospital in Iranische Strasse. The other letter was for Sophie Sara Berman and Meier Israel Berman, announcing their evacuation to Theresienstadt camp. They didn't take it too badly. It was known to be a model camp.[21]

On the appointed day they were all taken away in a lorry. Some wooden steps helped the old people to get aboard. Being a deferred armaments worker, I felt secure enough to travel with them aboard the truck. I also accompanied Aunt and Uncle up to the first floor of the assembly point in the Grosse Hamburger Strasse. A room was allocated to them there, where they had to wait. The beds had old mattresses without bedclothes; no table, no wardrobe. Nothing. Then Aunt realized that she had forgotten to bring the jacket of her dark blue suit. 'No problem,' I said, and went off to fetch it. I left the assembly point unhindered, and came back with the jacket. The policeman at the entrance nodded to me. He was obviously under the impression that I was a trusty steward. Later I left again with the same ease.

Now I was alone. All the rooms in the Münzstrasse flat had been closed off with a Gestapo seal. All except my room and the kitchen. The alarm clock on the two soup plates continued to wake me every morning. The work alternated from week to week as ever between day and night shifts.

Towards six one evening I was on my way to the Alexanderplatz S-Bahn station to catch the train to work. I walked round the large circular lawn, remembering what my father had told me about 1918, when the Germans went through something of a revolution. Shooting was going on in one corner of the Alexanderplatz. But the Berliners did not take the shortest route, straight across the lawn. Not at all; they ran round it. Why? Because there was a sign that said KEEP OFF THE GRASS.

In front of the formerly Jewish-owned Hermann Tietz department store a young man stood looking at the window display. I knew him! Det Kassriel, my former workmate – the little tailor. 'Det, lad, how are you doing? What are you up to?' 'I'm tailoring and living illegally.' 'Where are you living illegally?' 'At home.' 'Hm, that's not exactly the best hiding place.' 'It's the best I've got.' 'Then you might as well move in with me. I've got a large flat all to myself now. The others have been evacuated. You'll be all right with me. At least they won't be looking for you there.' The next day Det arrived with a big suitcase, and we began our semi-legal life together.

Graphic artist wanted

I pedalled along on the rickety bike my cousin had left behind when he made his timely escape to New York. Past the Schlossplatz, along Unter den Linden, through the Brandenburg gate. From there I continued under air-defence camouflage nets with artificial fir trees to the Victory Column. Then a left turn into Hofjäger Allee. Then on into Budapest Strasse, past the Romanisches Café where Erich Kästner, Kurt Tucholsky and Mascha Koleko used to sit arguing through the night. Finally, round the Memorial Church to the Kurfürstendamm. Turning into the seventh side street, I got off my bike in Bleibtreustrasse and stood outside the building where Thesi Goldschmidt lived, the mother of the girl from the commercial college.

Frau Goldschmidt enjoyed a 'privileged mixed marriage',[22] and lived in the exclusive west end of Berlin – but at the back of the building. It was a really genteel area. Nobody would have suspected there was a rear block here. To keep up the air of gentility, the path to the staircase ran through a garden, which even had a little fountain. Thesi Goldschmidt was half a head taller than me. I guessed her shoe size would be between eight and ten. She had a large nose. Her voice was husky. But her black eyelids had long silky eyelashes.

'Come in, young man,' she said as she opened the front door and, almost simultaneously, the door to her living room. 'I wrote to you because I have a job for you. After you were so bold about asking for the Sigmund Freud book back, with your hands stuck in your pockets, I told my friend that you were the right person. My friend wants to sell a microscope. And she's looking for someone to offer it to a private clinic for her. Would you take on something like that? I work as a nurse for a doctor and I know what a valuable instrument it is.' 'Frau Goldschmidt, I'm honoured by your faith in me, but I would really have to think very hard about it. The people in the clinic aren't going to buy a microscope from someone they don't know. I would have to produce identification and explain where the instrument came from.' 'Well said, young man. I thought the same all along. Now, as you're here, why not stay for some tea? Instead of the microscope I'll show you something else that will interest you.'

It was a General Staff map of southern Germany on a scale of 1:25,000, with the line of the Swiss frontier clearly marked on it. 'If we have some tea together, we can look for a border crossing point at our leisure. Would you like to do that?'

It was raining. After the night shift, Walter Heyman was waiting for me out on the street, under his big umbrella. He looked short next to the *Wehrmacht* soldier guarding Gustav Genschow's factory.

'Well, Schönhaus, you were asking me last time why the Jews are persecuted.' On the way to the station he held up the umbrella to cover both of us. 'I told you it was because we worship an unseen God. That makes us strong – but also weak and vulnerable. An abstract God is superior to all idols. It's significant that abstract art is banned under every dictatorship. Those in power don't know what lies behind it. What's more, if you believe an unseen God is taking care of you, you feel invincible. There's a good reason why it says on every German soldier's belt buckle "God with us". But there's also a dangerous side to this Jewish conviction of being the only people to have the unseen God behind them as an ally. Millennia ago the Jews developed a false view of the real world. And when they felt strong enough with their God behind them to wage war on Rome, the world power, they were defeated. And that's why we've been banished ever since antiquity. And in times like these we fight for our survival.'

Prompted by the word 'survival', Heyman went on: 'You were at applied art college. You started your training as a graphic designer. I know a woman who puts everything into saving Jews from deportation. This woman is looking for a graphic artist to help her forge a pass. Do you think you could do it? Would you like to contact her?' I agreed, and he explained: 'The woman is Edith Wolff. She is the daughter of a former editor of the *Berlin Tageblatt* newspaper. He was my boss. Her address is 79 Kaiserallee.'

Next morning, after the night shift, I went to see her. Her mother gave me a cool reception. Her father shut the door of his office as I entered the house. Obviously, neither of them was enthusiastic about their daughter's activities. But Edith Wolff, known to everyone as Ewo, greeted me with a radiant smile. She was small and insignificant-looking, and wore nickel-rimmed glasses. Her eyes had something chameleon-like about them. They looked in two different directions. Her hair looked as though she had cut it herself. But when she started talking, she came across as the kind of person who knows their own mind exactly. We went into the kitchen, where her friend was waiting for me. He introduced himself as Heinz (Jizchak) Schwersenz. His glance was penetrating, and his speech was rather hurried. But Ewo was in control of the situation.

It was a matter of substituting the photograph on a *Wehrmacht* discharge certificate and restoring the stamp that ran across the photo. In other words, the challenge was to imitate the official state eagle with its twelve large and twenty-four small feathers, and everything that went with it, in the right colour, with the right shape, in such a way that the stamp would stand up to any official scrutiny.

'Do you think you could do that?' 'I'll try. I've never tried it, but I reckon I can manage.' 'And what do you want for it?' 'Nothing. Well, maybe just one thing . . . Herr Heyman told me you have a room where people can hide if necessary. I don't need it yet, but I might do soon. I would be grateful for the address of the room.' 'Hmm, so Heyman passed that on to you . . . Yes, it's a small maid's room at our cleaning lady's place. She's called Frau Lange and lives at 29 Taunusstrasse. Yes, the room is in great demand. But if you need it, I'll make sure you get it.'

How to forge a stamp

I was fired up by Ewo's commission. I could finally offer some resistance. At last I didn't have to just look on helplessly at what they were doing to us. I got down to work that same evening, at my desk at home. It was the desk from whose drawer the Gestapo man had taken my father's wedding ring and slipped it into his waistcoat pocket. So this was the task in hand: to change over the photograph on a *Wehrmacht* discharge certificate and forge a replacement stamp across the new photo.

Using a magnifying glass, a fine Japanese brush and

watercolour paint, I copied the eagle and swastika from the stamp on the original pass owner's photograph, in exactly the original shade of purple. Then I took a sheet of newspaper, licked a blank piece to make it damp, and pressed it down on my watercolour copy of the stamp. The damp paper absorbed the paint, creating a mirror image of the stamp. All I had to do then was press the damp newspaper with the negative of the stamp on to the correct corner of Schwersenz's photo. Next, I fixed the new photograph in place with the old eyelets: the pass was complete.

I could hardly wait to deliver the forged pass. Ewo was quite taken by surprise. She had never imagined that the new photo and its stamp would look so flawless. From now on, with this pass, Schwersenz was no longer a Jew. 'You can have the room at Frau Lange's whenever you want. And there's

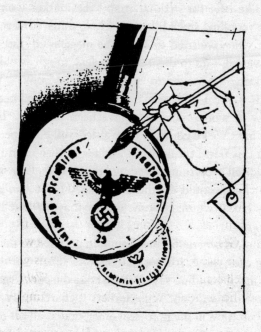

another thing: Dr Franz Kaufmann in Halensee is looking for a graphic artist, too. I'll give you the address. Go and introduce yourself. There's a lot to do.'

Dried mushrooms hung on a thin string in our larder. Det was standing in an apron at the cooker, rhythmically stirring a casserole with a wooden spoon. We were having mushroom soup garnished with finely chopped parsley. The quality of Det's soups would have won acclaim even served at the Hotel Adlon. Next to the kitchen table, we had pinned up a map of Germany, covering the whole wall. We used about thirty drawing pins. Where was the best place to cross the frontier? Towards Sweden? Switzerland? The choice was limited. But the soup tasted even better while you dreamt about it. Especially when you came back from work exhausted.

One day Det brought home a joint of wild boar. 'You prepare it like beef for making soup,' the market woman had said. The cooking smell filled the whole stairwell of the building. But when we tried to carve the meat, even our sharpest knives were not up to the job. 'Hopeless, tough as old boots,' fumed Det. 'We ought to buy a cookery book.' 'Yes, but money is tight,' I said. 'Since my pay got docked because of that row at work, our funds have been very low. But, you know what? We've got stuff from three well-equipped households in this flat. I think we should try to turn it into money. We could sell everything standing around here. Our old drayman, Richard, could do the deliveries. He's a haulier now. Det, my lad, if we make some money that way, we'll split it between us.'

Det looked worried. 'I need time to get used to the idea of flogging everything. It's not that simple. What will the other tenants in the building say? What about the concierge – she's also the block warden. Will Herbert Richard really want to come in on it? Will my market women take it all off me?' 'It's not going to be easy for me to get used to it either, Det. But I think we should take it one step at a time. First we'd better see whether we can get the Gestapo seals off the doors and stick them back on again. Yes, look, it works like a dream with warm water and a sponge.' Det was amused. 'The Gestapo are going to be so disappointed when they find an empty flat. I'll take some soundings in the market and see if it will work.'

One morning a new man turned up at Gustav Genschow's. Introducing himself as Friedrich Görner, he clicked his heels loudly. Heinrich Heine described this type a hundred and fifty years ago: 'They stride about so stiff and straight, so smartly dressed and groomed, as though the rod they once endured they afterwards consumed.' Friedrich Israel Görner was exactly that type. He was a qualified metalworker, who could file much better than I could. But there was one thing he could not do: he could not grasp that he was supposed to be a Jew. It was some time before I noticed the star on his jacket.

Friedrich Görner was taciturn, and he worked doggedly. Now and again, though, his shoulder twitched. During one night shift he told me his story, blinking constantly as he talked. He had taken part as an NCO in the invasion of France in 1940. He was awarded the Iron Cross First Class, and put forward for a commission as a result of his bravery. And then fate struck. All he had to do, 'just as a formality', as his colonel said, was to provide proof of his Aryan lineage. But the old church registers showed that both Friedrich Görner and his wife had Jewish grandparents, and were therefore classified as 'mixed race of the first degree'.[23] So Görner had to hand in his uniform. 'It's terrible,' he said. 'You wake up in the morning thinking it was just a bad dream – and then realize it's all true.'

When a German workmate brought him a bag of apples for his little girl, one of the others, Herr Kalkreuter, commented: 'It's no good feeling sorry and helping that Jew. They've brought their troubles on themselves. The war is all their fault. They've been cursed with blood guilt ever since they crucified our Lord. You can always tell a Jew. You can see it with Görner; the way he keeps on twitching and blinking – typically Jewish. That's his bad conscience at work. I can spot a Jew a mile off just by the way he walks. Even from behind. I find it weird that the army took so long to realize he was Jewish. And now you're giving the Jew apples for his kid. You're beyond help. Watch out that they don't come for you too one of these days.' Görner went on filing away, as if he couldn't hear what was being said behind him.

Det came back from the covered market with some bacon rind and a packet of sauerkraut. 'Our idea has fallen on fertile soil, Cioma. The ladies are dead keen on what we have to offer. They've all got plenty of money, and most goods are unobtainable. Come on, let's make a list. There's stuff here you can't get for love nor money these days: bed linen, table-cloths, silver cutlery, Grandma's jewellery, crockery, pots, pans, irons, umbrellas, carpets, cupboards, beds, mattresses, eiderdowns, trunks, suitcases, fur coats they didn't hand in, that fold-away Singer sewing machine of your mother's. I'm going to put a list together and go on the hunt!'

'But Det, one day they'll come to clear out the sealed rooms.' 'Then we'll tell them the authorities have already collected everything.' 'Let's hope they believe it.' 'Well, that's when we disappear like lightning. And when it comes to disappearing, there's a place we can go to – Frau Lange's room in the Taunusstrasse. Edith Wolff promised it to you.' 'Yes, Det, but you should see it. "Room" is an exaggeration. It's the sort of thing they kept for serving girls in the old days. There's no space for anything except the bed – not even a cupboard.'

'I know a fashion studio in Fasanenstrasse, Cioma. Now and again I get orders from the owner, Frau Zukale; I'm sure she's a safe bet. If we take Grandma's big wardrobe round and

The portrait of Herr Lehmann. I had it reproduced for the album I was going to show to Herr von Weizsäcker.

promise her she can keep it when we're out of the picture – I'm certain she'll play along. And in the meantime we can store our clothes and things there. I've hinted at the idea a couple of times to her, and she gave me the nod.' 'Det, you're an amazing chap! And if we can pay, I bet she'll mend anything that needs patching up, and let us wash our shirts as well.'

While we sat at the kitchen table discussing our strategy, the bell rang. Who could that be? If it was the Gestapo, our fine plan was scuppered from the start. I quickly stuck the seals back on the doors. When we opened up, there was Herr Lehmann. He unpacked his rucksack in the kitchen: he had sausage, Swiss cheese and real coffee. We let him into our plans and he immediately became our first customer, offering cash for the dining-room lamp if he could take it away immediately. Then he noticed my portrait of Grandma. 'Did you paint that? Yes? I want you to do a picture like that of me!' He put down three hundred-mark notes on the table. 'Payment on account.' But he wanted his portrait done there and then!

'But it will take a couple of hours, Herr Lehmann, and the Gestapo could turn up here at any moment.' 'All right, Herr Schönhaus, let's get started, then.' He sat down in an armchair. 'Time is something I brought with me, and I'm too old to be afraid of the Gestapo.' 'Actually, I've got to get to bed now, Herr Lehmann. I'm on night shift and I'll be working from six in the evening until six in the morning.'

'You are young, Schönhaus. Your friend can make some strong coffee, and you can make a start! Then I'll come back tomorrow afternoon, and we'll go on working like that till the picture's finished.'

Illusions

Yet another new colleague had joined us at the workbench – Manfred Hochhäuser. He was tall, and walked with a permanent slight stoop. Instead of wearing blue overalls like everybody else, he had a light-brown jacket. Against that background, his star was less conspicuous. He had an elegant command of German; you could see he had enjoyed a good upbringing. Görner told him his story. Manfred listened attentively and said rather condescendingly: 'We'll see, perhaps I can do something for you. I've got some pretty good connections.'

Görner and I wanted to know more, and constantly pressed

him. But Manfred Hochhäuser was very reserved, and any snippets of information emerged only gradually. Apparently, he had lived with his parents, both doctors, in a villa on the Heerstrasse. Their neighbour was Baron Ernst von Weizsäcker,[24] under-secretary of state in Ribbentrop's Foreign Office. As a child, Manfred had often played with the Weizsäcker children, whose garden was right next door. Since that time he had been a close friend of the daughter of the family. In fact, they were promised to each other and intended to marry eventually. It was only the 'race laws' that stood in the way.

During the quiet night shifts, when foreman Ackermann sat with his eyes closed in the darkness of his glass-screened office corner, pretending to supervise us, Manfred Hochhäuser disclosed his secret bit by bit.

'I won't be staying here with you much longer. I'm due to be aryanized. Baron von Weizsäcker has started the process already. You've got to remember that Field Marshal Erhard Milch[25] was originally a Jew, and he is now one of the top men in the *Luftwaffe* simply because Reich Marshal Hermann Goering said "I'll say who's a Jew and who isn't." So Weizsäcker can certainly arrange for me to be aryanized. All right, it means I'll have to join the army, but I don't mind that. Besides, von Weizsäcker told me recently that once the aryanizing business is over he'll have me made an ensign, which means I'll soon become an officer. The thing I care about most is getting officially engaged to Gudrun von Weizsäcker.' Then he showed me a photo of a blonde girl. 'That's her. Read what it says on the back.' It said 'FOR MY MANFRED'.

Once he confided to me: 'When we're on day shift the Weizsäckers send over their chauffeur-driven black Mercedes to collect me for dinner. There are often celebrities there. Yesterday it was Hans Albers with Karin Hardt,[26] and Albers told us the latest political joke: "A woman goes into a fish shop and asks for an Adolf Hitler herring. The shopkeeper shakes his head and asks her to say again what she wants. They haven't got any Adolf Hitler herring. Then the woman shouts: 'Well, surely you've got a Bismarck herring, haven't you? Yes! So, just take the brain out of the Bismarck herring, open its gob wide, and you've got your Adolf Hitler herring.'" Everybody roared with laughter. Yes, I must say, I'm very much at home there.'

Friedrich Görner blossomed. The possibility of being aryanized raised the curtain on his blacked-out life. Manfred Hochhäuser acquired an aura that made him seem sanctified.

'If you've ever got a problem, I can help you in various ways. You, Schönhaus, for example; you often have trouble getting in on time. I've got a couple of medicines my parents gave me: one brings on a fever, so that any doctor has to give you a sick note immediately. And then I've got the antidote, which stops the fever. Actually, I've still got lots of medicines from my parents' practice. When in need, just call on me! You can have pills from me any time.' 'All right, Manfred, but where are you living at the moment?' At first he didn't want to tell us. Then, reluctantly, he said: 'At 88 Pestalozzistrasse, with my grandmother. Just for the time being, though, till the aryanization thing goes through. When my parents were evacuated, von Weizsäcker was away on an official trip, otherwise he would have prevented it. I was in hospital at the time; that's why I was left behind. But now he's going to do something for me, and he wants to get my parents back from Poland, as well.'

I was impressed by the aryanization business, and I asked him if Ernst von Weizsäcker could do anything of the sort for me. 'I can't promise anything. But you're a good graphic artist. I'll take you with me to dinner there some time, and you can show him some of your work. Perhaps he'll think you're someone worth rescuing. If you like you can wait for me next Monday at seven under the clock at Savigny Platz station. I'll come and pick you up with the chauffeur in the black Mercedes.'

If I was going to display the photos of my graphic work properly, I urgently needed an attractive album, so I went to a leading bookbinder's on the Kurfürstendamm and ordered one bound in vellum. 'You can have it in a fortnight.' 'For goodness sake, I've got to show it to Herr von Weizsäcker next Monday evening!' When the bookbinder heard the name Weizsäcker, her face lit up. 'In that case you can collect the album on Friday.'

In my dream, bells were ringing close to my ears. 'This is the last day you'll spend as a Jew. Tomorrow Baron von Weizsäcker is going to open the gateway to a free life, without a star. You'll be a German, just like the people all around you.'

I rubbed my eyes. It was 8.30. The alarm had rung, but I hadn't heard a thing. Never mind; I might not be aryanized by that evening, but I would have the fever pills from Manfred Hochhäuser. Any doctor would have to declare me sick. So I strolled in a leisurely way to the photographer's shop which had promised to have the reproductions of my oil paintings of Grandma and Herr Lehmann ready for that day. The pictures were going into my album. Von Weizsäcker was supposed to say: 'Goodness, this fellow is damned talented; I must save him.'

I walked to the S-Bahn station at Savigny Platz. There was a bench under the clock, but I preferred to walk up and down. The Weizsäckers' villa was on the Heerstrasse, as Hochhäuser had told us. Anybody coming from that direction would have to turn right from the Bismarckstrasse into Grolmanstrasse. That's where he'd be coming from. And there he was: the black Mercedes. Driving slowly – but driving right past me, towards the Kurfürstendamm.

After that there was a delivery truck with a wood-fuelled engine, then an open-topped white sports car driven by a lieutenant, at his side a blonde girl with windblown hair. A Prussian prince, for sure, and no doubt she was called Dorothee. But the black Mercedes had still not shown up.

It was nearly half past seven. I was freezing, although it wasn't even cold. Perhaps the Baron had had second thoughts? I went to No. 88 Pestalozzistrasse. 'I live there with my grandmother,' he had said. HOCHHÄUSER was on the nameplate next to the bell. Above it there was a normal Jewish star: black on white paper, instead of on yellow cloth, the sort now found at all Jewish premises.[27] I rang, and a white-haired lady opened the door. 'Is Manfred here?' 'Yes. Why?' she replied hesitantly. And, after a pause, she added: 'What has he been telling you?' My mouth went dry. 'Was his father a doctor? And his mother?' 'No, why?' And then Manfred arrived. He stood there looking sheepish. His head was sunk below his shoulder blades, and the shock of hair hid his face.

Coldly, I couldn't help saying: 'Tell me, have you got the fever pills and the antidote?' No answer. Should I . . . No! He looked so pathetic. Wouldn't it be better to offer him my hand, and say: 'You are a victim of the criminals who have made you the pathological genius of a liar you are.'

But the ground had opened up beneath me, like a trap door under a man condemned to hang. I was falling into a void. I walked slowly down the stairs. A cool wind was blowing in the street.

'What is to be done?' is the title of a pamphlet by Lenin, written when the Bolsheviks were looking for a way out of an apparently hopeless situation.

The appendix operation

I needed a doctor's certificate to say I was ill. Otherwise I would have been absent without leave from Gustav Genschow's, and that would be a case for Herr Rensing, the Gestapo official.

A doctor. Who would know a doctor? Of course – the mother of the lovely Eve from the commercial college! She was a nurse, and lived in Bleibtreustrasse, which was only ten minutes from where I was. I set off.

'Frau Goldschmidt, thank God you're at home. I need a doctor's certificate to say I've been ill today and couldn't make it to work.' 'Slow down, young man. We'll get this sorted out. I work for a doctor, and he's a reasonable man. But first we've got to work out how to go about it. Have you still got your appendix?' 'Yes.' 'Well, that's something, at any rate. Here's what we can do. Just a minute, I'll phone my boss.' She was already talking into the mouthpiece: 'Excuse me, Herr Doktor, it's an emergency. Probably appendicitis. Just what I thought, no time to lose. We're coming straight round to the surgery.'

Before we set off, she issued instructions to me: 'So, my dear Schönhaus, we're going to act out a case of appendicitis. I'll explain all the symptoms, so that the doctor is convinced. Show me your stomach. The appendix is here in the middle, between the navel and the groin on the right hand side. If I press down on that spot, it doesn't hurt. But if I take my hand away quickly, that's when you scream "ouch!" That pain is a symptom of an inflamed appendix. It also hurts when you pass water. Remember that. Now you know everything. Let's go.'

When we arrived at the surgery, I had to stretch out on the

examination couch immediately. The doctor pressed on exactly the right spot. The moment he took his hand away, I shouted 'ouch'. 'Well done, Sister. Your diagnosis was correct. I'm reserving a hospital bed straight away. That appendix has got to come out without delay. And you, young man, turn over on to your stomach, and we'll give you a pain-killing injection. So, Herr Schönhaus, tomorrow morning at nine. Sister Thesi knows the ropes and will go with you.'

Out in the street she gave me her arm. 'Come along. You'll be feeling the injection soon, and you can't possibly go home. And anyway, we're already past the curfew hour for Jews. No, I'll take you back with me and make you up a bed.' 'I don't mind what they do to me; I just don't want to go under the knife.' 'Don't worry. We'll find a way round that as well. You can go and see my doctor tomorrow morning and tell him it doesn't hurt any more, and so you don't want to be operated on. Just ask for confirmation that it was an acute case of appendicitis, and that although you really ought to have an operation, you are taking responsibility for turning it down.'

Frau Goldschmidt put a mattress down on the floor for me. I undressed and got under the covers. My disappointed hopes in Baron von Weizsäcker lay like a stone on my chest. The briefcase containing the vellum-bound album lay on the carpet next to me. I was almost asleep when I heard her husky voice: 'Aren't you cold down there on the floor?' A light went on in my head, and I was immediately wide awake. She was a motherly woman; next to her I felt like a small boy. I had always enjoyed feeling like a small boy. I wasn't in the least nervous. She knew what to do. Afterwards I slept without dreaming.

I felt like a prince next morning when she brought me a breakfast tray in bed: tea, butter and fresh rolls. I felt strong. Confidently, I said to the doctor later: 'It doesn't hurt any more, so I don't want the operation.' I was just as self-confident when I went to the Gustav Genschow company medic and presented him with the doctor's certificate: 'Cioma Israel Schönhaus was obliged to be absent from work yesterday because of acute appendicitis.' The firm's doctor remarked: 'Mm, appendicitis?' He shook his head very slightly. 'Show me your tongue. Oh, yes – it's coated all right.' He smiled and signed. 'You are excused.'

At No. 11 Münzstrasse Det had been imagining the worst, as he was bound to do, in view of the fact that I had been away for a whole night. When I told him what had happened, he simply couldn't contain his astonishment. He scratched his head, chewed his finger nails, and finally had to laugh.

Suddenly dog tired, I went to bed. I had to get a little sleep in before my shift started at six that evening. I couldn't afford a second absence. But rather than getting the rest I needed, I dragged myself to Elberfelder Strasse, past St Saviour's Church, along Putlitzerstrasse, as far as the freight station. There was a miserable stream of more than seven hundred Jews surging along the road. At the Putlitzerstrasse station a goods train was waiting. There were makeshift steps up to the open doors. Everyone got on. Slowly. No one was cursing. Nobody was screaming. But at the front, near the puffing engine, a Jew was in dispute with an SS doctor. 'Listen, I was an officer in the Great War. I know how soldiers are transported in goods wagons. You just can't get away with what you're doing.' The SS doctor refused to be ruffled. 'My dear fellow, that's not all I can get away with.' He drew his pistol and pointed it at the head of the First World War officer. A shot rang out. The man's head made a cracking sound against the paving, like a clay pot. After the shooting everyone got on to the train more quickly. Then there was the sound of a pea whistle, shrilling endlessly, ceaselessly.

. . . until I realized that it was my alarm clock, standing on the two soup plates. I got dressed quickly. I could hear Det in the kitchen. He had made an inventory, and was engaged in discussion. Our attractive neighbour, the concierge and block warden, was sitting at the table writing, drawing up the list of things we wanted to sell. Whatever she needed for herself, she could have for nothing. So, at least within the building, our move out of the flat would now enjoy the best possible protection.

Dr Franz Kaufmann

Heyman walked along with me through Treptow Park, clutching his star. 'You know, Schönhaus, it's nothing short of a miracle that they believed your confidence trick about the appendicitis.' 'Why, Herr Heyman? Foreman Schwarz didn't believe me at all. When I showed him the certificate, all he said was: "That's not valid for me until our company doctor's confirmed it." And then he did confirm it.'

'You see, Schönhaus, it *was* a miracle. But what you've told me about Hochhäuser is the exact opposite – a chimera. I wouldn't tell poor old Görner anything about it, if I were you. Let him enjoy a few more happy days, while he still believes that aryanization is possible. You know, you can never rule out miracles, Schönhaus, but you shouldn't bet on them either. It's better to rely on your own efforts. What's more, you are in the fortunate position of being able to help others. You provided Heinz Schwersenz with a perfect identity card. Edith Wolff can't get over it. She thinks that with your talent you should be rescuing more Jews, and with Dr Kaufmann[28] you have a chance to do so.'

'Tell me more about Dr Kaufmann.' 'Dr Franz Kaufmann is

an extraordinary person. He was chief secretary of the Reich
Public Accounts Office, and a captain in the First World War.
He comes from a Jewish family, but was baptized as a child.
He's married to an aristocratic German woman. He's an
active Christian in the Confessing Church,[29] involved in helping Jews to escape deportation. He enjoys privileged status
because his wife is Aryan and he has brought his young
daughter up as a Christian. He doesn't have to wear a star,
and his ration cards don't have the "J" stamped on them. So
in practice he can lead the life of an ordinary German.
Nonetheless he chooses to run the enormous risks involved in
helping Jews. He puts all the courage of a heroic officer into
fighting for people who are persecuted and deprived of their
rights. He regards caution as a form of cowardice. As he sees
it, "If you want to capture an enemy trench, you can't afford
to be cautious; you've got to have the courage to look danger
in the face."

'Go and see him, work with him. But try to spell out to him
that careful plotting is just as important a weapon as heroic
courage. Otherwise, your life as a passport forger will be a
short one. Just think about it: anybody caught with an ID
card you have forged will be quizzed by the police about
where he got the pass, who swapped over the picture and
copied the stamp. There aren't many who can keep a secret
when their fingers are shoved in a door jamb and the door
slammed shut on them. Unless they really don't know anything, in which case there's nothing for them to give away.
That's why nobody must know your name or address. The
same goes for Dr Kaufmann.

'He's still the correct German official who hates anything
illegal – a German, in the best sense. Despite his illegal activities he is still the absolute soul of moral integrity. For
instance, God help you if, as one of his collaborators, you
were to ask for more than the one book of stolen ration cards

a month. He would be finished with you. If Hitler were not out to persecute and exterminate the Jews, many nationalistically minded Jews would be his faithful allies. But now he's in the process of bringing about his own defeat, in true paranoid fashion. We'll just have to watch out that he doesn't take us down with him.' Heyman's words put me in a deeply thoughtful mood.

It was three o'clock on a Sunday afternoon. The staircase of Frau Goldschmidt's building smelled of perfume, coffee and floor polish. I had been invited for coffee. She was uncertain how to behave towards me. 'Just call me Sister Thesi.' Then she invited me into her sitting room and put her arm round my shoulder.

There were two other friends of hers there: one was Tatjana Kober, a black-haired, vivacious Russian woman. During the First World War she had worked as a nurse in a military hospital under the command of the Tsar's daughter Olga. The other guest, Marie von Bredow, was a lady who had been drafted in as secretary to the military administration of Warsaw. Previously she had worked in the adjutant's office of General Johannes Blaskowitz,[30] before he wrote a memorandum complaining that the treatment of the Jews was endangering the discipline of his troops, after which he was penalized by being posted to the Netherlands.

Marie von Bredow was on leave in Berlin, and she had brought real coffee and Polish poppy-seed strudel back from Warsaw. The four of us sat around a circular drawing-room table. The coffee smelled like peacetime. The icing from the strudel dropped on to the dark blue carpet. Frau von Bredow talked with her mouth full as she told us: 'Children, you should see what they're doing to the Jews in Poland. I'm not allowed to talk about it, but I'll tell you one thing: make sure you don't get sent there.' 'We *are* making sure, as far as we can. Take our young friend here: he's about to go underground in Berlin. His parents have been evacuated. For the moment he's living with a friend in the family flat. They're in the middle of breaking up the household to make some money.' 'Just don't get caught. Have you at least got decent ID papers?' 'Yes, I'm a graphic artist and I can make my own.' 'Is your name Cioma?' asked Tatjana. 'That's a Russian name.' 'Yes, my parents come from Minsk, in Belarus.' 'Then we are fellow-countrymen. You say you're selling off the household? I'm looking for an electric iron. Have you got one for sale? Yes? Why don't you bring it round. Here's my card.'

The visitors had left. I took the crockery into the kitchen. There was a man there boiling water for tea. He looked like some kind of company director or something, used to having his tea made for him by an employee.

Later Thesi explained: 'That was Dr Meier, an extremely rich mill owner. He's got so many properties in East Prussia that he's convinced the war will be over before they can expropriate him; he's sure the Nazis will lose, anyway. The Meiers are well-educated, cultivated people. I talked to him about you and told him you're a graphic artist. He wants you to go and see him. He's got a job for you.' Dr Meier needed a special certificate from a local Nazi Party leader. He could manage the text himself, but he needed an official stamp.

At No. 11 Münzstrasse Det was stirring pea soup with bacon. I sat close by, at the kitchen table, copying the eagle stamp with the help of a magnifying glass; first of all the right way round, and then the mirror image. Finally, I dampened the back of the newsprint by spitting on it, and pressed it down to make an impression. The stamp was perfect; all it needed was a little touching up. There was no great art to it. However, looking over my shoulder, Det said: 'Yes, there is.'

'Just say my name is Rogoff.'

When I took him the certificate with the stamp, Dr Meier called his wife over. 'Just look at that. Can you believe it?' While Frau Meier was peering at my work through her lorgnette, there was a ring at the door.

'Herr Schönhaus, I'm expecting a visitor, an old Russian gentleman. How shall I introduce you?' 'Just say my name is Rogoff.' The visitor was pretty elderly. 'May I introduce Herr Rogoff?' The old man looked at me: 'Rogoff? Did you say Rogoff? Is your family from Russia?' 'Yes.' 'From Minsk?' 'Yes. Actually our name is Rogowin. But my grandfather called himself Rogoff.' 'Incredible. Just imagine, I knew your grandfather!'

Dr Meier's glasses practically dropped out of their frames. He thought I had just made up the name Rogoff on the spur of the moment. There followed an animated conversation about my 'grandfather's' timber business. My real grandfather had told me once about his timber merchant playing around with his name. At one time my grandfather had his own forest in Minsk, with its own railway. Rogoff, the timber merchant, was my grandfather's business partner; he was originally called Rogowin.

After the old man left, Dr Meier asked me how much I wanted for the stamp, and could see I was embarrassed by the question. 'You know what, I'll introduce you to somebody who will be very useful to you. You'll get more out of knowing him than anything I could pay you. Come over next Sunday afternoon. The man is called Ludwig Lichtwitz. You will be a perfect team.'

Ludwig Lichtwitz was a thickset man who smiled when he talked, and stumbled over his words because his mind raced ahead of his tongue. He came straight to the point: 'I'm going to show you something incredibly valuable. A genuine military passbook. Blank – that is to say, not filled in yet. I've got two of them. If you can complete one of them with all the stamps, you can have the other one. Could you do that?' Dr Meier looked at both of us expectantly. 'I could probably do it. But I'd need something to work from. I can't invent the stamps.' 'We'll have a word later about borrowing a service passbook from somebody. First of all I want to tell you about some opportunities we've got. I'm on friendly terms with the chauffeur from the Afghan embassy. His boss has given him permission to rent premises where Jews can hide. So, on behalf of the Afghan embassy we've rented a former greengrocer's in the Waldstrasse. We've painted the windows white on the inside. Now the space is officially a workshop and stock room for electrical supplies belonging to the embassy.'

'But what made you choose electrical materials, Herr Lichtwitz?' 'Well, old friend, there's a third partner involved here – Werner Scharff.[31] I'll tell you some other time about his speciality. I suggest we meet the day after tomorrow at 54 Waldstrasse. Is that OK? We've got a lot to discuss.'

At No. 11 Münzstrasse practically nothing was left unsold, except for the kitchen table and two mattresses. Det had invited in his market women with their friends. Our attractive neighbour helped us to take careful note of all their addresses, and next day haulage contractor Herbert Richard and his brother-in-law delivered everything. All this time I was still living legally in the flat, going to work punctually at Gustav Genschow's.

But one thing we needed if we were going underground was ration cards. The only person we could get them from was Dr Kaufmann, if all went well. That was why I was sitting on the tram on my way to Halensee, to visit him there in Hobrechtstrasse.

His elegant villa stood in a large garden stocked with old trees. When I rang, a tall blonde woman opened the door. 'My name is Schönhaus. I've come to see Dr Kaufmann.' 'What do you want?' 'I was recommended by Edith Wolff.' 'My husband is out. Just go away.' At that moment Dr Kaufmann himself appeared behind her. 'I gather Ewo sent you? Come in. I've been expecting you,' he said in a kindly manner. Then his tone changed, and suddenly he was the complete chief secretary. 'Leave us alone, please,' he said, in a voice that was used to giving orders.

He led me into an old-fashioned study with heavy leather armchairs, smelling of stale cigar smoke. Without a word, he went over to a bookcase and brought out a sewing basket containing balls of wool in various colours. Underneath them were a number of identity cards – official German passes. 'You see, people put these passes into the collecting box at church, instead of money. They run very little risk, because losing ID papers is not a punishable offence. It can happen to anybody. Look, I've got passport photos here of Jews about to be deported to the east. With a German pass like this they're safe when they're stopped in the street. If the card fits the owner in terms of sex, age and photo, then the strictest check in the world can't harm a hair on their head. I'm giving you one of these passes, Schönhaus. Make a sample for me. If it's good, I can get you a lot of work, because the need is great. And tell me, how much would you charge per pass?' 'At the moment, nothing. We've got plenty of money from the sale of our household goods. What we do need, though, is ration cards. Ewo said I could get one book a month from you.' 'That's true. But you said "we"?' 'Yes, a friend and I are going underground together.' 'All right, then, you can have two books a month. And when will I have the pass with the new photo in it?' 'The day after tomorrow, at the same time.'

I went with Det to Taunusstrasse to show him the maid's room. The front building was enormous, five storeys, with three flats on each floor. We reached the back building, which was just as big, by crossing the inner courtyard. On the second floor there was a nameplate under the bell push saying MATHILDE LANGE. Frau Lange was a dear little old lady with white hair; very German. When she opened the door to show us the maid's room, I was glad we had deposited Grandma's massive wardrobe in Frau Zukale's fashion studio. The room was minute.

Det was full of enthusiasm. The room was good. He decided we shouldn't ask Frau Zukale to pay for the wardrobe, because this hideout was priceless. Now there were no more obstacles. We had disposed of the three households, and shared the money equally. And we had illegal accommodation. We had been promised ration cards. Det urged me to burn my bridges and give up working. 'Believe me, one day they'll round up all the Jews at Gustav Genschow's without warning, and evacuate them. Then it'll be too late! Didn't you tell me yourself that they're training up more and more Dutch and French workers? Why do you think that is?'

All the same, I had good reason to hesitate. For a Jew as for anybody else, it was one thing to be legal, registered with the police, officially resident in a flat with an address to which post was delivered – and quite another thing to be unregistered, an outlaw, having to look out for yourself in a lawless zone, living according to your lights. The bourgeois love of order runs deeper than you realize.

There was another reason why I hesitated – the thought of having to share a bed with Det gave me the shivers. But then chance came to our aid. I lost my ID card, which I had to renew every three months at the police station. I had already lost it once, just a short time before. Reporting its loss again so soon would be tempting fate. We rummaged around everywhere, in pockets, briefcases and drawers, but with no luck. It had simply vanished. The die was cast – for good and all, I had to go underground in Berlin.

Whenever I was in trouble, I tried to feel close to my father. Werner Schlesinger, who had been in prison with him, to whom he had given his last piece of bread, was still living legally in Berlin. So I went to him. He opened the door of his flat and asked me to wait in the hallway for a while. Before five minutes had passed, a young woman came along the corridor. Her make-up was showy, and her dressing gown couldn't conceal a stunning figure. Nonchalantly she asked me if I could lend her a handkerchief, as she had a terrible cold. I gave her my hand-kerchief, and promised to bring something for her cold from the chemist's next day.

When Werner Schlesinger came back out she had disap-peared. 'That's a fantastic woman you've got living with you!' 'Listen, I'm going to talk to you like a father, Cioma: don't have anything to do with that girl. Yes, she's my cousin, but she's got a terrible character. She's just twenty-two, and living illegally with a German sergeant. With no papers. And what's more, when her partner is away on active service, she's always picking up other men. She'll come to a bad end.'

Next to me, Friedrich Görner was at his workbench, busy filing. 'Schönhaus,' he whispered, looking around to make sure no one was listening, 'my only pleasure in life now is your trick with the hammer. As many rejects as I like.' The left side of his face twitched from time to time, and now and then he gave a laugh, talking to himself and shaking his head. 'Look at him standing there, that Manfred Hochhäuser. Standing at his bench filing away as though nothing has hap-pened. And yet he ought to be struck down dead, the filthy liar. But other people will take care of that for us. They'll take care of everything for us. Everything!'

Görner did not know it was my last day in the place. I said goodbye to Heyman. 'Herr Heyman, I'll miss our walks through Treptow Park. Let me have your address, though.' I told him about all the preparations I had been making, and also about my visit the day before to Werner Schlesinger and the immoral, seductive cousin he had warned me against.

'Schönhaus, your father's friend is right, but he's also wrong. Morality is for people living an orderly life. When you can't plan for the future, as we can't now, it's only the present moment that counts. Of course, there are people who would stick to the straight and narrow path even in hell itself. But they are the exceptions. And it's only after the event that you can tell whether you're one of the exceptions. We don't know what the future holds for this young girl, or for any of us. The point of life is to live it. Some philosopher once coined the phrase *Hic et nunc* – here and now. How you are judged morally doesn't matter. Moral norms are constantly changing over time. But what you've got to do is avoid unethical behaviour. What I mean is, don't hurt anybody. "Do not do unto others what you would not have done to yourself." You see, these are quite simple rules to follow.'

Gerda

Werner's lovely cousin was called Gerda. Two days later, we sat next to each other on white-lacquered chairs outside the Café Kranzler on the Kurfürstendamm, waiting for our banana milk shakes, even though at any moment an army patrol might come up and demand: 'Young man, can we see your service passbook, please. Why haven't you been called up?' There is an earthy saying in Berlin: 'When your cock stands to attention, your reason rushes to your arse.' Gerda looked even prettier in daylight; all the men turned round to look at her.

I told her about my plans, and how little I was looking forward to sharing a bed with Det. 'You can sleep at my place,' she said, 'but only from Friday onwards. My husband's on leave until Thursday, then he's got to go back to the front line. So you can come over on Friday. I live in Steglitz. We'll have to be very careful, of course; a lot of people know me there. My husband is a sergeant, and he always carries his army revolver on his belt.' We slurped our banana milk shakes.

'Perhaps it will be safer if I don't come until Saturday evening?' 'All right. I'll be waiting at eight o'clock on the corner of Steglitzer Strasse. It will be dark by then.' I gave her my arm and we strolled down the Kurfürstendamm to the underground station.

The Münzstrasse flat sounded as hollow as a church. All the rooms were empty. The souls of the owners were far away as well – perhaps already in heaven. Only the kitchen table was left, apart from the electric iron reserved for Sister Tatjana. Next to it lay a letter from the Jewish Community Association of Berlin. I opened the envelope. 'You have not complied with our request that you should present yourself here in connection with leaving your accommodation. We must point out to you that you are obliged without fail to appear at the time appointed by us. For the last time, we invite you to attend at 10 a.m. on 30.9.1942. If you fail once more to keep this appointment, the severest measures will be taken.' I didn't take this letter seriously, either.

Det came into the kitchen, grinning: 'Hey, Cioma, do you know what day it is today?' 'Oh, Det lad, today is the 28th of September 1942. Do you know, that's the first time I've ever forgotten my birthday.' 'Well, I haven't forgotten it, Cioma, and neither has our attractive neighbour. We've been invited next door. She's made a special cake for you. You're twenty today.'

Det had put two bottles of *Liebfrauenmilch* wine in the neighbour's fridge. She was waiting for us in her living room. All the furniture looked very familiar. 'So, at last we can raise a glass,' she said, toasting me. 'My name is Ilse. I think it's a real shame you can't go on living here for ever. But I hope Det, at least, will come round and see me now and again.'

Next morning there was no hurry about getting up. At last I could have a proper sleep, since I was not going to work. It was my first day as an illegal. I felt as though I was playing hooky from school.

We moved in with Frau Lange. Our small suitcase contained only pyjamas, toothbrushes and washing things. Suits, coats, shirts, underwear and socks, and everything else left in the drawers, had been dropped off at Frau Zukale's place. I took my forgery tools in a leather briefcase, as well as the ID card that was going to be my showpiece, and the photo I had to re-mount.

Frau Lange greeted us like a nice old grandmother. After we paid the rent advance agreed with Edith Wolff, she became even friendlier. And when Det asked if he could make some coffee, since he'd brought real coffee with him, Frau Lange's enthusiasm practically knew no bounds. The three of us drank our coffee in her kitchen. Afterwards she let me use the big dining-room table to work on my ID card. My work had to be convincing, not only for Dr Kaufmann, but also for the policemen who would be checking out the document's owner.

Frau Lange was only worried about one thing: 'What am I going to tell my son when he comes home on leave? He might not agree with me putting up Jews. And I'm expecting him in the next few days.' 'Frau Lange, if he's your son and you've brought him up, then he's bound to be like you. I'm sure we'll find a way to sort out the sleeping arrangements. Whatever the future holds, fear is always a bad ally.'

Dr Kaufmann was expecting me at six o'clock, and it was already five. I wanted something to eat first, and went to a stylish restaurant on the corner of the Kurfürstendamm and Karlsruher Strasse. A man standing in front of it turned round, shrugged his shoulders, and walked away. On the door, a notice said CLOSED. Underneath was written: 'I charged extortionate prices, and that is why I am now in a concentration camp.' Signed: Secret State Police, Berlin.

Oh well, I thought, the Nazis are making sure that neither my money nor my hatred for them run out. The pub on the next corner was more modest. The menu in the display case next to the entrance included a country-style omelette, with fried potatoes and ham. My favourite! I ordered a glass of light beer with it. What more could I want? It was delicious. While I was eating I thought: 'If I'm ever condemned to death, and they ask me what I'd like for my last meal, I'd order this omelette and a light beer. After that, nothing would bother me.'

Dr Kaufmann's villa, set in elegant parkland, could easily have been some professor's private clinic. A few magazines lay on the coffee table in the study, where five Jews were waiting, planning to go into hiding in Berlin. Dr Kaufmann received me in his office, seated behind a desk. I had tucked the forged ID card away inside a folded newspaper, where it would not be immediately spotted in a body search. Student-style, Dr Kaufmann rapped the desk with his knuckles in appreciation. 'Good idea, that business with the newspaper. You're right: you've got to use your head.'

He took the pass, went to the window, said nothing at all, and left the office. I could hear somebody next door thanking him. Then I saw a man walking out through the garden towards the road. 'You see, Schönhaus, you never met him.

That's my principle; the people you make passes for will not know who you are. Then, if it comes to the worst, they can't betray you.'

All the visitors had left. He took out his sewing basket from under the bookcase and handed me five more passes, with passport photos to match. He added two more books of ration coupons and declared: 'I'm happy with your work, Schönhaus. I am appointing you my assistant. I'll see you next Friday at the same time.' And then, as though he sensed my misgivings, he went on: 'Our system has been carefully worked out, you know. What happens in a police check? Somebody is stopped in the street and ordered to produce identification. At worst he is taken to the police station, where they check out whether the owner of the pass is registered with the police. If he is, then they establish whether he's wanted for any offence. If he's not, they let him go. Schönhaus, it's possible that my villa and the apparent normality surrounding my rescue operations are a better way of going about a conspiracy than if I were to meet every one of my protégés at night in a dark place. The Gestapo are not trained in criminology, so, like the man in the street, they think illegal activities only take place under cover of darkness, with the participants going around in turned-up collars looking furtive. My style is the exact opposite, so I don't fit the Gestapo's preconceived ideas. That's what keeps us safe.'

All the same, I knew that on any visit to Dr Kaufmann a Gestapo man might open the door to me. I felt as though I were playing Russian roulette every time I went there.

Dr Kaufmann was satisfied with my first forged pass. But I wasn't. Once opened and re-closed with pliers, the eyelets fixing the photo to the pass no longer looked absolutely right. What I needed was the sort of tool used by cobblers to fit eyelets for shoelaces.

It occurred to me that our former shoemaker, Hans

Marotke, was bound to have that kind of punch. I knew his basement workshop in Dragonerstrasse very well because he sold and repaired bicycles as a sideline. My cousin's bike, which I was now using, came from his shop.

Marotke was an old Communist: you could trust him with your life. When I asked him whether I could use his eyelet-punching machine occasionally, he replied: 'I can imagine what you want it for. But don't do it here, if you don't mind. Make your ID cards at home; I don't want anything to do with it. I'd rather sell you the old machine. But don't ever let on where you got it. If things really go wrong and they insist on knowing where the machine came from, just say you pinched it off the truck collecting scrap iron. You can give me fifty marks for it.' Wrapped in brown paper and tied with string round its middle, the machine was a handy shape for tucking under your arm.

I went on to visit Ludwig Lichtwitz in his shop in the Waldstrasse. We had arranged that I should knock seven times. The Waldstrasse was actually more of an avenue than an ordinary street, with maples growing along the promenade in the middle. No doubt this was where the residents strolled in the fresh air on Sundays, with or without dogs. On one side of the road was the terminus of the No. 11 bus. Its destination was Friedenau, but that doesn't matter for the moment: the double-deckers stood empty, dozing as they waited for passengers. The illegal shop, its windows whitewashed on the inside, stood only about thirty paces away from where the bus drivers stretched their legs. In the gateway to its left lay hundreds of rolls of electrical cable. Next to them stood cardboard boxes full of light bulbs, stacked head-high, and endless lengths of telephone wire.

I knocked seven times, and Ludwig opened up. He looked well rested, and as though he was suppressing a smile. After double-locking the door, he showed me his illegal kingdom.

On the wall to the right hung an enormous cupboard full of all sorts of hardware: pliers, spanners, files, saws, nails, screws. 'All just a front,' said Ludwig.

There were two sofas standing on end, leaning against the wall. 'You see, I've already sorted out somewhere for you to sleep.' 'Wonderful; then I won't have to share a bed with my colleague at Frau Lange's any more.' 'Hold on, don't get carried away, Schönhaus. We haven't got running water or a lavatory on the premises. Both are outside in the courtyard. You can't sleep here for long; just one or two nights at most. But there's one thing you *will* be pleased about: I brought a small desk from my printing shop for you. For your work and for the military passbooks – once I've found the right models to copy.'

'I've brought something for the desk drawer as well, Herr Lichtwitz: an eyelet-punching machine.' 'Fine, but the other drawers are reserved for my stamp collection, Schönhaus. That's my hobby, and also my investment for the future. Look at these Polish stamps, all overprinted with "German Generalgouvernement". After the war these stamps will be valuable. During the day I scour the stamp shops buying these occupation stamps for a song. They're limited issues.'

'And what about all that electrical stuff in the entrance to the building?' 'That's all part of our disguise. All the tenants think that, if a little workshop like this can be so well supplied with electrical equipment, when everything is rationed, then it must be all right. A neighbour asked me recently what we actually do here. "Military secret, dear lady," I said, and she asked no more questions.' 'But where do all the electrical supplies actually come from?' 'From my friend Werner Scharff. He's our third man, after you.' 'What sort of person is he, then?'

'Werner Scharff used to maintain the electrics in the Jewish Congregation building in Berlin. The Gestapo have

107

requisitioned the whole place, and because the Jewish electrician, Werner Scharff, gets on well with the Gestapo
officials, they've kept him on there. He knows the wiring
throughout the building, of course, so now he's the resident
electrician for the German authorities, which gives him practically unlimited access to electrical supplies. That's ideal
camouflage for us, and for him it's something laid by for
after the war.'

'I may be the youngest musketeer, Herr Lichtwitz, but I'll
do my best to come up to scratch. I'll be here every morning
at eight o'clock sharp, if I can, and I'll put on a white overall –
I've still got one. I'll look like a technical draughtsman. That
will impress the neighbours, and help to complete the camouflage effect.' 'Good, but I'm not giving you a key, Schönhaus.
For security reasons it's always kept in the hole in the wall
under this stone. You just have to make sure nobody sees you
putting it back. See you tomorrow at eight.'

Then came the first night in Frau Lange's maid's room, with
Det and me sharing the bed. To avoid touching him, I made
myself as thin as I could. I lay there without sleeping, eyes
open, my mind playing on Saturday evening at eight. 'I hope
she'll be at the corner as planned. I hope nothing's cropped
up.' And finally I dropped off to sleep.

Saturday arrived, and she really was there. Could somebody that pretty want *me*? I couldn't believe it. She acted as
though she didn't know me. Then she moved her head very
slightly to indicate the direction. I followed her until she
stopped outside a five-storey apartment block. A few steps led
down from the street. She looked around, and opened the
door of a neat one-room flat.

The heating was already on. Hanging on the coat rack
were a rather sweat-stained felt hat, an army cap, an overcoat and a thick pullover. Some well-worn slippers lay on
the floor. On the left was a double bed, and on the right, in

the corner, a washstand with a mirror, and a shelf for scent bottles above it. It smelled of Evening in Paris. Off to one side was a cooking alcove. 'OK, I'll make us something to eat.' She put some water on to boil and reached for the macaroni. 'Yes, I love that, too,' I said, although my mouth was very dry; it would be hard to get anything down. She ate very heartily. I had my mind on something altogether different.

After washing up in leisurely fashion, she began to undress, as though it was nothing out of the ordinary. She lay on her back across the bed, dangling her legs, and waiting. I had never seen such a beautiful woman naked. My heart was in my mouth. 'Get undressed and come here!' Then what Stendhal says happens to every man befell me too. 'Oh, come on!' she repeated.

I had put on such experienced airs for her, acting the self-confident man of the world. And now? 'You bore me,' is all she said. She found her nightdress and slid under the bed-clothes. 'Let's get to sleep.' I lay next to her, once again with wide open eyes, but the fantasies of the night before were a thing of the past.

When the first rays of the sun shone into the room round the drawn curtains, she took me in her arms. 'You're a little show-off, aren't you. You're not usually afraid of anything. Why are you so frightened with me? I'll show you how it works.'

The time that followed was timeless. I had ration coupons, I had money. I did the shopping, she tidied up and cooked. She washed her hair and varnished her nails, always in the nude, humming from morning till night the hit song 'You Shall be the Emperor of my Soul'. In bed I traced her contours, feeling the thoughts of the men who turned round to look at her bouncing off me. And all this in the bed of a German sergeant travelling towards the front, while goods trains full of Jews

trundled towards death. Everything that was happening around me made life surge twice as strongly through my veins.

'You must live, my boy. For our sake.' And 'What's going to happen . . . don't think about it . . . don't think about it . . .' 'Why is your heart beating like that?' asked Gerda.

The paper I am writing on now suddenly smells of Evening in Paris.

I had a night off from Gerda, finding the prospect of sharing the bed at Frau Lange's not as dismal as before. In any case, I had to give Det his new book of ration coupons. As soon as I got to the staircase I heard a gramophone playing the aria 'On With the Motley'. There was a pair of dirty army boots standing outside the door. So the moment that Frau Lange feared had arrived. But I heard Det laughing, and knew it couldn't be too bad.

Frau Lange's son was a broad-shouldered youth with a childish face. He sat there with his uniform jacket off, his braces over his collarless shirt, and his feet in grey socks stuck out in front of him. With a broad grin, he gave me his hand. 'So, you're the third person in our trio. You can't believe how much I envy you boys. Out there in all that shit, I'm always dreaming of doing a bunk. But you two have actually done it, and you're living in my old bedroom. Will I ever come back again? And if I do, will I still be in one piece? I wanted to be a singer and go to the conservatoire. But all that's left now is my records. I'm glad you like listening to this sort of thing. Hey, lads, meeting you here calls for a celebration. We'll go into town later for a drink.' Frau Lange was beaming. She hadn't imagined her son's leave could be like this. All her fears had vanished completely.

We went from pub to pub in the darkness. At first we sang two-part army songs. How could any policeman suspect that hidden behind those bawling lads were a couple of Jews living illegally? After the third beer he began to tell us: 'You can't imagine what's going on out there. Especially with the Jews.' From a secret compartment in his wallet he took out some photos that made underground life in Berlin seem like a picnic. 'I tell you – just don't let them catch you! Have you at least got decent passes?' 'Yes, look, I've got a post-office ID card. It gives my name as Peter Schönhausen. Det's got one too.' 'But it'd be even better if they didn't take too close a look at you.'

The nights I spent with Gerda were making me more self-confident all the time. But my dreams were haunted by what I'd seen in young Lange's photos. I saw long rows of Jews being shot. I heard the shots: one, two, three, four. Then another two. Gerda woke me up. 'There's somebody knocking. Can't you hear it? Wake up. It's my sister-in-law. She's always dropping in for coffee. She brings the coffee with her.

Curl up and get under the bedclothes, and she won't notice anything. But you mustn't move an inch. I'll push your clothes under the bed. God help you if she tells her brother I've got someone else here.' The knocking went on. 'I've got to open the door now.'

I have never sweated so much in my life. Even worse was the lack of air. I could hear scraps of conversation from outside; what people were saying about Stalingrad, and how much you had to give for a pound of real coffee nowadays. Both women chatted away cosily. I thought Gerda was a little *too* cosy. I lay there curled up like a cat. A fly had taken refuge with me under the bedclothes and was crawling up and down me. I didn't move. How long does such an eternity last? Finally I heard the door to the street opening, then closing again. At last I could breathe a sigh of relief.

An orderly existence

I always delivered to Dr Kaufmann at six on Friday evenings. I now regularly took him about ten or a dozen passes in my folded newspaper. I had refined my technique; the demand was great.

I had developed a pattern for Fridays: at around five I ate in my pub at Halensee. All I had to do was nod when the landlord asked 'Country omelette again?', and my favourite meal was served up – with a glass of beer, naturally. By six o'clock precisely I was ringing Dr Kaufmann's doorbell. The chief secretary (retd.) insisted on military punctuality. The garden was so big that the neighbours could hardly see who was coming and going. So I thought, anyway.

I felt important when, through the half-open door, I heard his commanding tones: 'My dear Frau Kommerzienrat, I can't settle this by myself; I'll have to consult my expert.' He showed me an ID card. 'As you can see, this belonged to a middle-aged lady. It all fits nicely, except that her occupation is given as "chambermaid".' Against all the rules, the lady herself now appeared in the room. 'Herr Doktor, I'm the wife of a managing director. Anyone can see I'm not a chambermaid. The occupation must be changed.'

True enough, with her snow-white hair she looked the part of an elegant lady. Her husband's title of 'Kommerzienrat' (commercial counsellor) was probably conferred on him by Kaiser Wilhelm, and adopted by her, too, in the old-fashioned German way. The chief secretary (retd.) asked me whether I could change the occupation on the identity card. 'No – forged handwriting is very easy to spot. It will make the pass useless.' 'Frau Kommerzienrat, you've heard for yourself what my expert has to say. There's nothing we can do.'

Despite her misgivings, Frau Kommerzienrat set off on her travels with the ID card and tried to escape into Switzerland. I had surely made the right decision. But wasn't there a touch of callousness in my attitude, an outlook which the Nazis had implanted in everybody, us Jews included?

Two weeks later I heard what had happened. Not far from the Swiss border, in a forest near Ramsen, Frau Kommerzienrat was arrested by two German frontier guards. As the three of them were on their way to the guard post, one soldier asked the other: 'What have we got here, anyway?' 'Oh, just a chambermaid, that's all.' 'I tell you what, mate – why don't we just let the old dear go?' So Frau Kommerzienrat came back to Berlin and told Dr Kaufmann: 'Herr Doktor, being a chambermaid saved my life.'

Before I left, I was handed my ration book. Then I was allowed to stay while Dr Kaufmann put his little girl Angelika to bed. She was about three years old. Every night he had to carry out exactly the same ritual: it involved a teddy bear, a donkey, a pony and a puppy. The stern Dr Kaufmann made all these stuffed animals dance on the cot rail. First came the bear, and then the donkey. The pony rode on the donkey and the puppy on top of them all. In the end they all tumbled down into little Angelika's cot. Only then would she go to sleep. Frau Kaufmann was a benign onlooker at this ceremony. I was slowly drawn into the life of the family.

By now I was practically taking for granted the nights I spent with Gerda. My life was almost an orderly one. In the mornings I went to Ludwig Lichtwitz's shop and worked at my small desk, completing my daily quota of passes. One day, with the aid of a patent liquid preparation from the Pelikan company, I discovered a method of erasing all the writing from a post-office identity card. This opened up new prospects by enabling me to fill in the whole of a pass, from A to Z.

One day Gerda and I were having lunch at a restaurant which offered excellent speciality dishes without ration coupons; very often huge Dutch oysters, accompanied by an Alsatian *Gewürztraminer* wine. It was expensive, but I had a fat wallet, after all. After we had eaten like royalty, I went to pay the bill – but where was my wallet? In my jacket? My briefcase? My blood ran hot and cold. While I was thinking what to do, Gerda was eyeing me icily, with a look that said: 'You shouldn't carry your entire fortune around with you. Don't raise your hopes; you won't get anything out of me.' I was thinking hard. Where had I last used my wallet? On the tram? To pay our fares? Perhaps it had been handed in at the lost property office. It not only contained all my funds, but my forged post-office ID card[32] as well.

At the tram depot the official reached into a drawer, produced my wallet and asked: 'Is this yours?' 'Yes!' 'How do I know it's yours, though?' 'My identity card is in there, and it's got a photo.' He looked inside. 'Well, you're in luck, I must say.' 'Thank you. Here's fifty marks reward for finding it.' 'Come on! That's far too much.' 'No, no, just keep it.'

I went back to the restaurant to find Gerda still sitting at the same table. But a Waffen-SS soldier had taken my place. He got up when he saw me, and his parting words were: 'So, till next Monday evening, eight o'clock.' Then he left, ignoring me.

Gerda claimed that befriending an SS man would make us both safer, but from then on, I slept in Frau Lange's room with Det: Werner Schlesinger was right, after all. On the surface I was impressed with myself for finishing with Gerda so quickly, but inwardly I had no idea how to fill the void in the pit of my stomach. The abrupt end to this first love was hard to bear, even though I knew how unwise the affair had been.

The philosopher Immanuel Kant had a servant called

Lampe. For years he carried out his duties to the full satisfaction of his master. But one day Kant discovered that the servant had been stealing from him. He dismissed him instantly. No sooner had Lampe gone than Kant began to miss his services badly. Eventually Kant distributed little notices throughout the house saying 'forget Lampe'. So I hung up little messages everywhere in the rooms of my mind: 'forget Gerda'.

Hunting for rooms

It was dark. The clock in Frau Lange's dining room was striking eleven, and I was lying in our single/double bed, making myself thin and dreaming. Suddenly the door to our maid's room creaked, and Det crept in. 'Good, you're not asleep. Listen, something really stupid happened to me last night.'

To avoid giving away our hiding place, we always came back very late to Frau Lange's, when the street was empty, so that there was no chance of anyone entering the building at the same time as we did and noting where we lived. 'Last night a man walked into the hallway alongside me,' confessed Det. 'God knows where he sprang from. All of a sudden, there he was. He stayed next to me as I crossed the courtyard to the rear block. He followed me up to the first floor. I didn't stop at Frau Lange's door, of course, but went on climbing the stairs, hoping the man lived on the next floor. But no; he carried on as well. I got to the third floor, and so did he. I was hoping he would finally open a door and go in. But it was no good; he just went on. By then I was on the fifth floor, and so was he. So I just carried on. He stopped, and asked: 'Hey, where do you think you're going?' 'To Frau Lange's.' 'But she doesn't live in the attic! She lives on the first floor.' 'Oh, I must have made a mistake.' He shook his head, and watched me making my way downstairs again. Cioma, I think I've given away where we're living.'

'I doubt if it's that bad, Det. But we'd better look for another place, all the same.' Det thought of Frau Zukale. She had our wardrobe, and he thought he would be all right there; he got on very well with Frau Zukale, and would be able to tailor for her.

But I would have to think of something else for myself. Then I remembered that in one of the Zoo station arcades there was a shop window with a notice saying ACCOMMODATION OFFICE. I went there the next day. There was a long queue at the counter, but finally it was my turn, and I told a fictitious tale: 'My uncle was bombed out in the air raid before last on Cologne. I've been called up for military service from next Friday. I need a room for four days so that my old uncle can have my bed.' Even as I spoke, I was wondering how the woman behind the counter would react. She didn't react at all. With a routine air she gave me a list of twenty addresses, adding coolly: 'Next please.'

Now I had to test my story in reality. At seven that evening I crossed the Nollendorfplatz into Motzstrasse, where I rang a bell marked EBERHARDT on the first floor of a large block of flats. A sporty-looking woman opened the door. 'I've come about the room.' I told her the story about my uncle, and how I was going into the army on Friday. She looked at me sadly. 'My boyfriend is on active service, too. I wish you luck for the future; you can certainly have the room meanwhile. But you'll have to register with the police, even though it's for such a short time. You'd better do it first thing tomorrow; it's too late tonight.'

I slept wonderfully in the cool, freshly made bed. Next day I knocked at my landlady's room. 'I'm afraid I've got to leave again. My marching orders have arrived at home: they came early this morning, so I've got to report to Lichterfelde Barracks tomorrow.' She bit her lip: 'Yes, that's the way it goes these days. That happened to my boyfriend, too. So you won't be sleeping here tonight, after all?' 'No, I'll be sleeping at home for my last night. That's what my mother wants.' 'I can understand that. Well, all the best.'

It became a regular daily routine. By eight in the morning I was sitting at my forger's desk. My white overall made me look like a technical draughtsman, which in fact I was, because my stamps were little technical drawings. The passes were all finished by late morning. Then I went to Frau Zukale's fashion salon, where I showered, put on clean under-wear and a freshly ironed shirt, and changed my suit, as befitted a Prussian prince.

One day, I bought a small bottle of scent in a chemist's; the brand was N, for Napoleon. Sniffing at it, Frau Zukale said: 'If this scent was good enough for Napoleon, then you smell all right.' I was in an excellent mood, and decided to have lunch in the Hotel Esplanade. It was the right setting for me: whenever something took the Prussian aristocracy to the cap-ital, they dined at the Esplanade, not at the Adlon, which was only for the *nouveaux riches*. So the Esplanade was the place for me, too.

This was not my only luxury. Frau Zukale's salon was in what was called 'the garden building', the rear block, from which the way out to the street was through a mirror-lined hallway. A staircase on the right led to the front building, and hanging next to it, a brass plate read SISTER MARIA VON BREITENSTEIN, PHYSIOTHERAPIST. I had never tried anything like that before, so why not now? It seemed to me the appropriate thing to do before a meal in the Esplanade. I imagined Sister Maria as an elderly nurse. But the door was opened by an attractive young woman. Apart from her white cap, there was nothing nurse-like about her. 'You're in luck: I just happen to be free. But in future you must make an appointment at least a week in advance. All right, get undressed. And now lie down over there. Shut your eyes and let your chin drop. Good. Can you feel how relaxing that is?' Hardly had I shut my eyes when ghostly writing began to appear on the wall opposite: 'Cioma. Behave yourself!' it read. 'She's a princess, you know.' Yes, but what about me – aren't I a prince? 'Yes, but even a prince has to control himself.' Otherwise there's a scandal. What was it my father always said? 'Man proposes, God disposes.'

Smirking, the princess threw me a white towel. 'So – now you'll have no trouble turning over on to your stomach; it's time to do your back.'

I got dressed and stood at her desk to pay. She looked me in the eye: 'Right, next time you come, call me about ten days in advance. Here's my card with my phone number.'

I floated hungry but contented down the road, my steps as light as if the pavement were cushioned on air. The commissionaire at the Esplanade opened the ornate door to reveal chandeliers, white-covered tables, liftboys, assistant waiters, waiters and head waiters. Sparkling glasses, thick red carpets. The waiter who ushered me to my table slid the chair forward for me as I sat down.

All of this was in keeping with my confidence-trickster act. The one thing that bothered me was having to share my table with an odd fellow-diner: perhaps he was an illegal like me? I found him disturbing. He slurped his soup and read the Berlin *Morgenpost* newspaper, while breaking off bits of crispbread from a packet he had in his pocket, and carelessly letting the crumbs fall on the carpet. Finally he left, and I breathed a sigh of relief. 'Have you finished, Herr Generalkonsul, or will you be returning?' asked the head waiter as he was leaving. 'Aha,' I thought, 'so that was a consul-general.'

It was late in the afternoon when I got to my next accommodation address. An old man opened the door. After listening attentively to my story, he went silently to a Victorian desk and with a trembling hand pulled out a police registration form. 'Fill that in and take it to the police station, then I'll show you the room.' 'OK,' I said, 'but the office will be closed by now. I'll do it first thing in the morning.' Once again I slept in a freshly made bed.

And so it went on, from one address to the other. Because I always arrived late in the afternoon, it always worked when I said: 'The police office will be shut by now. I'll go first thing tomorrow.'

The next door I rang at was opened by a tall woman with blonde hair scraped back into a severe knot. She scrutinized me with watery blue eyes and listened sceptically to my story. A uniform jacket of the National Socialist People's Welfare Service, a swastika armband round the sleeve, was hanging on the coat rack. She called to somebody in the living room: 'Horst, come out here a minute. Someone wants the room.' A dark-haired man with a little moustache under his nose appeared. He was wearing black riding breeches and high boots, and the impression made by his uniform cap was still visible on his forehead. Obviously he had just come off duty.

I repeated the story about my bombed-out uncle. The longer I talked, the more his face lit up. 'You see,' he said, 'if every national comrade behaved as sensibly as this man, we'd have fewer problems after air raids. Go and show him the room.' To me he said: 'You can register tomorrow morning.'

So it went on, from room to room. I had now ticked off nearly all the twenty rooms on the list. Meanwhile, I paid Dr Meier another visit. He thought my method of room-finding much too dangerous. He had heard from Sister Tatjana that she had a place for me, a good one. I ought to go and see her. Tatjana welcomed me warmly. One of her patients was prepared to let me have a room, she told me. She was a likeable young woman, living a secluded life with her mother in an isolated, patrician-style villa in Grunewald. I could stay there for nothing until the end of the war. She gave me an address in Hubertusallee; they would be expecting me next evening at seven.

I packed pyjamas, a toothbrush and my mouthwash. Then I took the S-Bahn train to Grunewald station, on the so-called 'Gold Coast' of Berlin. It really was a dream villa. The woods began immediately behind it. I could not imagine better accommodation for an illegal.

The gravel of the garden path crunched under my feet, and I was greeted like a friend of the family by the young woman. 'Let me have your coat, and I'll introduce you to my mother straight away.' The mother came in, and without looking in my direction at all listened to her daughter: 'Mother, this is the young man I want to give a room to. He's a Jew threatened with evacuation to a camp in Poland. We heard recently on the BBC what goes on there.' 'Are you mad?' replied the mother harshly. 'We've got neighbours. You know what they do to people who hide Jews. There's just no question of it!' To me she said: 'Get out of here! And go quickly!' I felt quite sorry for the daughter. But once again the message was clear. Don't rely on other people; fend for yourself.

Next morning I was a technical draughtsman again, pass-forging at my desk. For lunch, I went to high-quality restaurants, precisely the places where you would least expect to find a Jew living underground, and in the late afternoon I went back to scanning the list of rooms from the Accommodation Office. Eventually, though, something turned up that I had been hoping for all along.

A landlady in Kleiststrasse, with a good-natured face like a countrywoman's, listened to me attentively. 'Well,' she said, 'if I understand you correctly, you're registered in the normal way with your parents at home.' 'Yes, I'm registered with my parents.' 'And that's where you get your ration coupons?' 'Yes, of course.' 'All right, so why should I register you here as well? There's no need.' 'If you say so.' 'That way, I can save on the tax, too.' 'If that's what you want, I've got nothing against it.' 'Good, young man; here's the key.' For the first time in ages I slept as well as I used to at home in my own bed.

The sun was shining when I woke up. The window was open, and the tulle curtains were billowing into the room. I made the bed myself. In general I tried to behave like a well-brought-up son. I left no limescale marks on the bathroom floor. Aunt Sophie would have been pleased: I was the ideal tenant. At breakfast I talked about my work as a technical draughtsman, and about my colleagues. But what I actually did was a military secret, I said. I gave out that I hoped to be deferred, and avoid the call-up for the time being, because of my reserved occupation.

I reported to Ludwig Lichtwitz both on my let-down in Grunewald and my success in Kleiststrasse. 'How many addresses have you tried out now using your method, Schönhaus?' 'No. 7 Kleiststrasse was the eighteenth.' 'Cioma, I must say I admire your patience.' 'Not at all, Ludwig, it isn't my patience. My father is behind it somewhere, as always. His stories and his example still point the way for me.' 'How?' 'In 1917, when he was a young man in the Red Army, he was standing in St Petersburg station when he saw a big crowd. They were all shouting "Hurrah", and soldiers were carrying a very old woman in a red armchair through the station concourse. "What's going on here?" he asked the bystanders. "Don't you know who's arrived? That's the aristocrat Brezhko-Brezhkovskaya. She was banished to Siberia for twenty years. For twenty years she asked the guard: '*Sevodnya revolutsya?*' (Is it the revolution today?) And for twenty years the answer came back: '*Niet.*' Every day she repeated: '*Sevodnya niet, tak zavtra budyet!*' (If not today, then it will be tomorrow!) And now the revolution is here. Can you see that train with the red flag stretching from the engine to the last carriage? That's the train that brought Brezhko-Brezhkovskaya from Siberia to St Petersburg." You see, Ludwig, it was the example of Madame Brezhko-Brezhkovskaya that taught me the power of patience.'

By the following Tuesday there was a new development, however. That evening I reported to my landlady: 'What do you think? My work is essential to the war effort. They can't find a replacement for me, so I can stay in Berlin. The firm is definitely going to ask for a deferral.' She looked at me sadly. 'I let your room a month ago to a member of the Croatian embassy, and he's coming tomorrow. I'm afraid you can't stay.'

But then, when I came home to the flat on Wednesday evening, things were looking brighter. 'Listen, I've had a word with my neighbour about you. You can move in with Frau Schirrmacher today, if you like. Her flat is on this floor. She's really keen to have you as a tenant. Do you want to know why? Because I told her such a lot about you, how you make your own bed every day and always leave the bathroom spotless, so that you are just no work at all. I also mentioned that you're registered with your parents and get your ration coupons there as well, so there's no need to pay a penny in tax for you. That was the bit that impressed her most. Anyway, she's already been to the block warden and got his agreement. Why don't you go across and see her?'

Frau Schirrmacher was an officer's widow. Her hair was pulled back severely in a bun on the top of her head. 'So, you're the nice tenant from next door.' She looked me over.

'I'd love to take you, but only under one condition: you must not be officially registered as living here. You're already registered with your parents, aren't you?' 'Yes.' 'Do you want to know why I can't take you as a registered tenant? Well, then my room would be put on the official accommodation list, and if you did get called up one day, the authorities would make me take somebody else, whether I liked him or not. You see, tenants like you don't come along every day. I've already talked it over with the block warden, an old Party comrade of my late husband's. As far as he's concerned, it's all agreed.'

I was taken aback by her kindness. 'You can have my bedroom, Herr Schönhausen. I'll sleep in the "Berlin room".[33] A Hitler Youth leader has the big room at the front, and the lady next door to him is a secretary in the Foreign Office. Are you really called Schönhausen, and not von Schönhausen, like our Prince Bismarck?' 'No, just Schönhausen, without the "von".' 'I've always wanted a son like you. I have no children, unfortunately. I hope we'll get on well together. And thank you very much for paying the rent in advance. I'll go and fetch a writing pad and give you a receipt, if you like. But actually I'd prefer we didn't put anything down in writing, if you don't mind – you know, because of the tax.'

Frau Schirrmacher wanted to invite me to lunch for the following Sunday, but I declined politely: 'The thing is, since my elder brother was killed at Stalingrad, my mother has become very attached to me. If I'm invited out on a Sunday, I have to tell her well in advance.' 'I understand that perfectly. Give your mother my best wishes.'

In everything I told her and in the way I reacted, I tried to construct an image of myself that those around me would find credible. I had to expect people to talk about me behind my back. The least inconsistency, the tiniest slip could provoke questions, leading to investigations. That was what I had to forestall.

I left for work punctually at half past seven each morning. This also made the right impression in the neighbourhood of the Waldstrasse, where our illegal workshop was situated. Punctuality meant respectability, particularly in Germany. By about ten o'clock I had done the best I could with my technique to make the daily quota of post-office ID cards and passes check-proof, and then I was free to take a trip out of the city.

It was only twenty minutes by S-Bahn to Pichelsberg on Lake Havel. Sitting in a comfortable upholstered carriage, I saw a goods train travelling on another line parallel to ours. The steam locomotive was slowly pulling countless wagons. What was it carrying? Was it Jews travelling to Majdanek to be murdered? What did an individual on that train feel like? Had he managed to clean his teeth that morning? What if somebody was forced to do his business in his trousers? If it was all sticky and smelly down below? Or if somebody vomited? They were all standing squashed up against each other in the wagons, like sardines in a tin. The journey took three days and three nights. Can anyone imagine how long a single hour spent like that must have seemed? Those released by death were the lucky ones.

'Pichelsberg station, everybody out!' I left the train and lay down on the grass in a forest clearing. In my heart I could not reconcile goods trains and comfortable carriages. How far could you stretch when you did the splits? Could you keep one foot in a train full of deportees and another in a sailing boat without tearing yourself apart?

The sky was a heavenly blue, and far below me white sails were reflected in the water of the Havel. The boats lay motionless, waiting. My ear was close to the ground of the forest, and I listened to its voice. Yes, the earth could speak. I hugged the ground and kissed it. The grass tickled my lips. But it wasn't the grass, it was my father's moustache. 'Cioma, can you hear me? Mama and I have some good connections here in heaven. We're protecting you. You are living the life we never lived. In spite of the goods trains you must say "yes" to life. As our representative you have a duty to experience all the pleasures we were denied. Do everything you enjoy, as long as it doesn't harm anyone else. Can you see the sailing boats in the distance? Let the wind carry you over the waves as long as God gives you happy days. Buy one of those boats, instead of just dreaming about it and carrying your money around in your wallet! A sailing boat is a safe place to escape to and a good excuse for getting away from Frau Schirrmacher on Sundays. Gather strength and contentment on the water, so that through your graphic talent you can help others to survive! That's why you are there. You are our chronicler. Write everything down. Your memoirs will make us immortal.'

The sailing boat

Still communing with my father in my daydream, I took the path through the forest down to the lakeside. Next to a small yacht marina there was a large notice saying PAUL BÖHM. 'So, you want to buy a boat. It's not that easy. There aren't that many for sale. Some owners don't use them because they are away on active service, but they're not in a position to sell, and others are conscripts who are based here, and who like to sail on Sundays themselves. But just hold on, let me think a bit. I reckon I could ask Paul Vogt. Come back on Saturday; he's always here on Saturday afternoons. The main thing is – what's in it for me?' 'Well, what did you have in mind?' 'I'd say a bottle of cognac, or a suitcase.' 'I can get you a suitcase.'

When a printer produces headed notepaper for a firm, he always keeps a few sheets for his archive. Ludwig Lichtwitz had owned a well-known printing works, and he still had a stack of headed paper from AEG, as well as some from the Temmler chemical works in Tempelhof. He couldn't get over his amazement; first there was my stroke of luck with Frau Schirrmacher, and now this madman wanted to buy a sailing boat! But he congratulated me, and gave me some AEG letter paper. Using an old typewriter, I wrote on it: 'Peter Schönhausen is employed by us as a technical draughtsman, and needs a suitcase for business travel purposes. Signed Adolf Faber, AEG Technical Department.'

I picked out a suitable suitcase in a leather goods shop near the Kaiser Wilhelm Memorial Church. Armed with my letter from AEG I had no trouble at the till. On Saturday afternoon Paul Böhm introduced me to the man who wanted to sell his boat.

Paul Vogt was an open-faced, sporty type. He held out a firm hand and introduced himself: 'Paul.' 'And I'm Peter.' 'Good, let's go and take a look at the boat, then.' It was sitting in the harbour, one of the smallest boats tied up to the buoys. The whole deck was made of mahogany, and it had a whip-shaped mast – 'it bends at the top,' explained Paul. 'Let me see your shoes. Well, at least you're wearing crêpe-rubber soles, though gym shoes would be better. Do you know your way around a boat at all? Have you ever done any sailing?' 'Yes,' I said. This was a massive fib, because all I had ever done was sail with Anton Erdmann. Never mind.

'And what about the financial side? I can't let you have the tub cheaply. I'm going to want at least two and a half. Can you manage that?' 'I think so.' 'Have you got the money on you?' 'Yes,' I said. 'OK, let's go for a little test run.'

First we went down a little canal, passing a small lighthouse as we reached the open waters of the lake, the Stössensee. As though the weather god had suddenly begun to puff hard with full cheeks, the sail filled out. The boat started to move, and the wire attached to the metal rudder began to vibrate with a deep hum. The faster the boat went, the higher the tone of the humming. She couldn't go too fast for me. Paul tacked the boat through the wind. I loved it. 'Watch out, for goodness sake! Move across to the other side or you'll have us over!' But we didn't capsize, and I told myself that sailing was child's play.

'You're a real clown,' Ludwig objected when I told him about my sailing adventures. 'What if you really had capsized, what would have happened then?' 'But yachts can't sink, Ludwig. They have buoyancy tanks to keep them afloat.' 'Yes, but the water police would have turned up, anyhow. And you would have had to show your papers. And I suppose the watercolour stamps on your post-office ID card are waterproof?'

'OK, Ludwig, in future I'll leave the pass in my locker in the boathouse. Would you like to come out for a sail with me sometime?' 'No thanks, you can count me out. I find life ashore dangerous enough as it is. Besides, I've had my fill of water sports. I used to own a motorboat once. But you can have my white trousers and white roll neck sweater, if you like. I could collect them from my wife some evening. I go and visit her now and again, although she has officially reported me to the police as missing. She's an Aryan, you see, and because we have no children our mixed marriage doesn't count as "privileged".[34] So they can come and deport me at any time. And that's why I'm here now.'

Fortunately, Paul Böhm didn't watch my first attempt at sailing, so he didn't see the clumsy way I cast off the boat. However, I would soon make friends with it, I thought. Its name was written in brass letters on the stern: KAMERAD. *Nomen est omen*, I told myself as I rowed out of the marina. At first, the water in the canal was quite calm, but where the small lighthouse stood, at the entrance to the lake, there was a much fresher wind. I tried to hoist the sail, but it wasn't even halfway up before the wind caught it and the boat was on the move. The boom lay across my knee, and I had to hold it with both hands; there was no time to tie off the halyard before the boat began to race along. On shore, I simply hadn't noticed the strength of the wind. The tone of the hum from the rudder wire was rising continually. From both sides spray dashed against my face. How would it all end, for God's sake? Was the Havel really that wide? It seemed to go on for ever. I steered with all my strength towards the opposite bank. Finally there was a crunch as the keel grounded, and I landed among the reeds.

Meanwhile, it had got dark, and the wind had dropped. The sirens rose and fell – an air-raid warning. This could get a bit tricky. Anti-aircraft guns started barking, and the white fingers of searchlights combed the sky for planes. When two of them locked on to the same aircraft, the din of the guns began in earnest.

Unfortunately, the shells fired into the sky did not stay there once they had exploded, but came splashing down into the water as shrapnel. Not on my head, please! It wouldn't make any difference whether I stayed in the reeds or rowed back; the splashes were everywhere. So I rowed back as it gradually got lighter. I arrived, soaked with sweat, back at the boathouse, tied the boat up, and took the first train home. Frau Schirrmacher hadn't noticed anything. I had a cold shower and arrived punctually at Ludwig's place. For the time being, I wouldn't mention to him what had happened. But after I had finished my quota of passes, I went out and bought a book: *Sailing for Beginners*.

Tatjana

Tatjana was born in 1889 in Siberia or, to be more precise, in Tomsk. She was Russian and looked the way you expected Russians to look: black hair, broad cheekbones, Mongolian eyes, strong teeth and slightly rounded features. When she talked she gesticulated, her eyes flashed, and she rolled her Rs.

She was angry about my frustrating rebuff at the elegant Grunewald villa. Her patient had expressly told her she wanted to shelter a Jew living in hiding, and then this affront happened. 'Don't be hard on your patient, Tatjana. It was her mother's fault.' 'All right, Cioma, to make up for it I'm going to invite you to supper, Russian-style. I want you to feel at home.'

The table was covered in all sorts of delicacies. Smiling up at me were red caviar, sturgeon, olives, salmon, butter and warm toast. Nearby stood an ice-crusted bottle of vodka. After the hors d'oeuvre there was borscht, real Russian blinis, and crêpes fried in butter and stuffed with a mixture of tender mincemeat, hard-boiled egg, chicken fat, bacon dripping and rice. She opened a bottle of Moët et Chandon. 'And now we'll drink to brotherhood, so we can exchange kisses.' I was not particularly good at holding my drink, and had never been really drunk. But champagne and three vodkas loosened my tongue. I talked and talked. So did she.

She claimed to be Jewish, but I guessed she had been baptized into the Russian Orthodox Church. I could see as much from the various medals and honours hanging on the wall in a small silver frame: she must have been a very courageous nurse. Tatjana was keen to introduce me to her circle of aristocratic Russian émigrés, but she found my Russian rather poor and there and then began to give me lessons. She also thought of a teacher, a certain Herr von Brezhko-Brezhkovsky. I asked whether he had anything to do with the famous 'Grandmother of the Revolution'. 'For goodness sake, don't mention that. As far as he's concerned, she's dead. He is a Grand Duke; he was a page at the court of the Tsar, and he's ashamed of his mother.' The supper was a protracted affair. To round it off there was 'charlotte russe', sponge roll soaked in vodka. Actually I wanted an early night, and as it turned out I got one, but not in my own room at Frau Schirrmacher's. Tatjana's breakfast was as luxurious as her supper.

The next evening, she insisted on taking me to the theatre in the Gendarmenmarkt, to see Gustav Gründgens and Käthe Gold[35] in *Hamlet*. The tickets were procured for her that same day by the cleaning lady in her building, whose husband was a stagehand at the theatre.

The streets were in complete darkness because of expected air raids. Whenever a window was lit up by mistake, instantly from below there came a loud chorus of 'Put that light out!' Pedestrians wore little phosphorescent buttons in their lapels to prevent collisions in the dark. But in the festively illuminated theatre, there were very few reminders that there was a war on, except for the many men in uniform. During the interval Tatjana led me to the buffet in the foyer, and as I was waiting for her glass of *Sekt* I heard her talking in Russian behind me. I turned round to see two officers in German uniform, whom she obviously knew. Afterwards she whispered to me: 'They are Russian aristocrats hoping to recover their estates when the Soviets are beaten.'

It was a world-class production. Naturally I took Tatjana home afterwards, wondering whether I still needed my luxury accommodation at Frau Schirrmacher's.

Returning dog-tired next morning to Kleiststrasse, I felt I owed my charming landlady an explanation. I took her into my confidence, confessing that I was having an affair with a woman twenty-four years older than myself. I begged her, in case my parents enquired about me, to tell them that I always went to bed punctually. If they found out about my much older girlfriend, there would be trouble. With an amused smile, Frau Schirrmacher promised to lie for me. Now we were more or less accomplices.

'But listen, Herr Schönhausen; there's something I have to confess to you. While you were absent for so long, and that young man from the Hitler Youth was away, too, attending a conference, I was utterly alone in this big flat. The Hungarian military attaché wasn't here either. I slept very badly, and had some terrible dreams. I dreamt that the Russians were coming, and the Jews. It was dreadful. It's a relief that you're back.' While she was speaking, the sirens began to howl: another air-raid warning. 'Come along, Frau Schirrmacher, give me your arm.' The dark steps down to the shelter in the cellar were steep. 'I'll carry your case.' In the cellar I told her about my adventures with the sailing boat, how I had been blown across the Havel by myself, and then had to row back at night during an air raid, with the flak splashing all around me in the water. 'Schönhausen, Schönhausen, the things you get up to. I'm so glad nothing happened to you.'

After the all-clear – it was another false alarm, just to stop Berliners from sleeping – I lay in bed reading, concentrating very hard on how to get a sailing boat started. Quite simple: you pointed the boat into the wind. When the sail was hoisted it was slack, flapping loosely like a flag. Only when you wanted to get under way did you steer the boat round a bit and wait for the wind to fill the sail and start you moving. Then you could steer wherever you wanted. I learnt how dangerous tacking was for a beginner, and how to tie a bowline so that the boat would not break loose from its moorings. I knew what I had done wrong last time. In theory, I could now sail a boat: but I could only take the boat out on Sundays, to avoid attracting attention.

I went to Ludwig's every morning as usual. Nowadays I usually had lunch at Kempinski's on the Kurfürstendamm, formerly a meeting place for high-class Jewish society in the west end of Berlin, and an establishment which, although it had been aryanized, still had the aura of a first-class restaurant. Now there were no more Jews; or, if there were any, they were like me. A young lieutenant sat with his mother at a nearby table. He was telling her about his experiences at the front: how his commanding officer, lying on top of a tank, had led them into the midst of a Russian column, and how, firing his machine gun from up there, he had halted the enemy's advance. He was bound to get the Knight's Cross for it. 'But, son, that's dangerous. I hope you don't do things like that.' 'Mother, we're soldiers.'

On Sunday, it was glorious weather for sailing. My yacht

moved along the Havel in the direction of Wannsee. With me were Hanni Hollerbusch, a half-Jewish friend of Dorothee's, and another 'half-Aryan' girl whom I knew from school days. We had a following wind. The mainsail was set to starboard, and the jib to the left. We lay at our ease in the boat on sofa cushions that Mama had embroidered with bright birds, flowers from paradise, and fantastic decorations. If she only knew where her cushions were today, and who was leaning so comfortably against the side of the boat . . .

Hanni Hollerbusch looked across to Nikolassee, where our friend Renate Klepper[36] used to live. We all stared silently in that direction as though transfixed. Then Hanni said: 'Renate took her own life.' And she began to laugh. She laughed and laughed and laughed. She could not stop until the tears were running down her face.

The wind had veered around. 'Over to the other side, everybody. I've got to avoid this steamer.' Still laughing, Hanni spluttered: 'Her father, her mother and Renate, they all killed themselves. Together. With gas. In the kitchen.' 'Hanni, what is there to laugh about?' 'I don't know. Looking at these cushions I can't help thinking how carefully your mother looked after them. And now they're lying here in the boat getting wet. And Renate. She was so cheerful. She moved like a dancer. And we're out here on the Havel.'

Hanni had visited my home once with Dorothee, and knew Mama and Papa and the sofa cushions. It went quiet on the boat. Nobody spoke. Hanni had known Renate right to the end. Her application for entry to Switzerland had been turned down, and she was also refused a visa to leave Germany – by the Home Office Minister, Wilhelm Frick, even though he knew her step-father, Jochen Klepper, very well. Now Renate was in a place where you needed no visa. The sky was cold, and it was listening. A seagull sat on the top of the mast, travelling with us. Was it Renate Klepper?

The Escape Artist

Dr Kaufmann laughed and patted my shoulder. 'Schönhaus, you know what I'm going to call you from now on? "The Escape Artist." First there was the room at Frau Schirrmacher's, where you weren't even *allowed* to register. And now this sailing boat business. Do you know what? You ought to start a school for illegals and pass on your expertise. Basically our activities are criminal. But under a criminal regime what we are doing is the only appropriate way to behave. Well, you're young, adventurous, and have a positive attitude to life. That's why you are successful. But I am a former chief secretary, and I have had to rethink a lot of things. Still, that keeps one young as well. Anyway, back to the business in hand. Here are eighteen passes and three post-office ID cards. Do you think you can manage them by next Friday?'

Next morning I arrived punctually at our shop. It was rather cool. Without taking my coat off I went to collect the *Thurgauer Zeitung*, the only Swiss newspaper regularly available in Germany during the war. When I got back, Ludwig had already lit the small cylindrical stove. It was crackling and throwing out sparks. I wanted to get down to work, so I looked around for the newspaper I had used, as ever, for carrying the passes inconspicuously. But the paper was gone. 'Ludwig, have you seen my newspaper?' 'Yes, why? It was from the day before yesterday.' 'Yes, but inside it were twenty-one ID cards that I got from Dr Kaufmann yesterday!' 'What? Oh my God, I've just lit the stove with it.' I went hot and cold. 'How am I going to explain this to Dr Kaufmann, Ludwig? And only yesterday he wanted to give me a title – the Escape Artist.'

I went straight out to Halensee. Dr Kaufmann gave me a penetrating look. His icy stare was hurtful. But there was nothing I could do about it. The more I tried to tell him how it happened, the less he seemed to believe me. And because I had so much respect for him, his distrust was deeply wounding. 'Do you know what an identity card fetches on the Black Market? Up to three thousand marks! Unless members of the Confessing Church deposit their passes in the collecting box, hoping to help someone by doing so. And you're trying to tell me your friend burned the passes by mistake?' None the less, he went to his bookcase, pulled out the sewing basket from under its bottom shelf, and gave me a few more identity cards. But this time it was only five. He wanted to reduce the risk.

Sister Tatjana had taken up a specialization in bee-sting injections for rheumatism. There was a certain Herr Jankowski who came regularly for treatment. I saw him often, because somehow I now belonged to the fixtures and fittings of Tatjana's flat. Jankowski was under forty, and looked athletic. Was he really suffering from rheumatism, or was he drawn to Tatjana for some other reason? Whatever it was, he trusted her. One evening, it all came pouring out: 'Tatjana, I'm suffering. I'm suffering because of my job.'

I sat astride a chair turned the wrong way round, with my arms on the chair back and my head on my arms. Jankowski opened his heart. 'You see, Tatjana, I work for the only agency in Germany responsible for Russians. I'm the first secretary in General Biskupski's office. When the police were looking in Munich for Hitler after his putsch attempt, he was sheltered there by a White Russian émigré, just for a few days. It was this tsarist General Biskupski. Hitler has never forgotten it, and after 1933 Biskupski was allowed to open a bureau for tsarist officers. A kind of government agency,[37] but only for Russians guaranteed not to be Bolsheviks, and of course not for Jews either. Now, suddenly, with Germany fighting in Russia, this office has become significant. All the former barons, counts and grand dukes – many of them now high-ranking officers in the *Wehrmacht* – hope to become the new masters of Russia. And I am secretary to the head of this agency. General Biskupski died five years ago, and Herr von Taboritzki is its current chief. Every day we receive letters. They break my heart.' Herr Jankowski was in tears. 'Russian women deported to Germany write that although they are pregnant they're forced to shovel coal out of wagons. They plead for lighter work. And what do you think I can do? Put a date stamp on them and file them, that's all. The Germans are heartless. I'd like to help – but how?'

I asked Herr Jankowski: 'What work does your office do, then?' 'Something very important – we issue passports. We carry out some very thorough research first, though: is the applicant Aryan? Where exactly was he born? What is his profession? His father? His military status in Russia? When did he leave the country? Where did he cross the border? Where is he living now? Has he taken out German citizenship in the meantime? What is his German military rank? Where is he working? What Russian church in Berlin or elsewhere does he attend? Has he produced satisfactory references? Marital status? And so on and so forth. It's a long questionnaire. Herr von Taboritzki asks the questions, and I fill in the answers. The applicant and Herr Taboritzki both sign it, and then a passport is produced, with a photo, fingerprints, and a precise description of the individual. One copy is kept in the office in case there's any follow-up.'

The longer Herr Jankowski went on describing his job, the more I wanted to own such a passport. I suddenly heard myself saying, very rashly: 'Herr Jankowski, you want to help. Would you help me? Yes, you did hear me correctly. My background is Russian, too. But I am a Jew. My parents came from

Minsk. They were deported in June 1942, and I'm living in hiding in Berlin. The kind of passport you issue could save my life!' Tatjana was horrified. 'Cioma' – when he addressed me by my first name, it was a weight off my mind – 'Cioma, I will help you. Just let me think how to do it.'

I slept badly that night, and Tatjana thought I had been very foolish, but nonetheless I was pleased I had asked him. I was sure he meant what he said. He came back the next evening: 'I think I know how to work it, Cioma. Can you give me a few personal papers? A statement from the factory you work for?' 'Yes, I can bring you something in writing on headed paper from AEG. Will that do?' 'Very well indeed. And then I'll need a police registration form.' 'You can have it. The form can be bought in any stationer's, and I can add the stamp myself. I'm a graphic artist.' I showed him the stamp on my own post-office ID card. 'So you've already got a pass, Cioma!' 'Yes, Herr Jankowski, but yours would be genuine. The first drop of rain would dissolve the watercolour paint on this stamp. And with your passport there'd be no problem about police follow-up at the office where it was issued. Right now, any enquiries at the post office would be fatal for me.' 'We'll manage it, Cioma. I'm developing a plan. I need four passport photos from you. I'll be back tomorrow to tell you how we can do it.'

Gradually Tatjana began to trust him. Over a light supper he explained how the procedure would go: 'When we inter-rogate applicants for a tsarist passport, Taboritzki sits at a large desk, usually in SS uniform: he's an Obersturmführer [First Lieutenant]. The applicant stands. I sit to one side at a small table and take down every word.' 'In Russian?' 'Of course!' 'But, Herr Jankowski, my Russian is hopelessly bad.' 'Just hold on, Ciomka.' He used every possible variant of my pet name. 'Ciomtschka, if all goes according to plan you won't see Taboritzki at all. The interrogation is a military one and Taboritzki is a pedant, in every respect, including eating. That's his weak point: every day he goes off at precisely ten minutes to twelve to the restaurant next door. They always keep a table laid for him. That's our opportunity! If there are still applicants waiting at a quarter to twelve, he usually asks me whether there's anything suspicious about them. If I say no, he signs the documents and says "just finish the business by yourself"; then he goes off punctually to lunch. When I've got all your documents, Cioma, we can fix a day. I'll fill in the long questionnaire myself, and you can wait in the waiting room. If I can see he's not going to go off punctually to lunch, I'll come out and say "it's too late today – come back tomorrow". But if things go as usual, you'll have your new passport in ten minutes.'

A few days later I was sitting in the waiting room at Taboritzki's bureau. I was the only one there. I had given Herr Jankowski my passport photos the night before. The ten minutes seemed endless to me. Then the door opened, and Jankowski came out. His official expression masked a smile. He gave me the passport. 'Come along, we'll just do the fingerprints quickly.' I thanked him, and felt as though I had been born again. I had taken a new Russian name: I was now called Peter Petrov. In case of a police or *Wehrmacht* check, enquiries could be made at Taboritzki's bureau. And the answer would always be: 'Yes indeed, everything is in order. Peter Petrov is properly registered with us. There's nothing against him on the record.'

Fortune oblige

Stella Goldschlag was a Jewish fellow-student of mine at the School of Applied Art in Nürnbergerstrasse. She was the

Marilyn Monroe of the girls there, and I would have liked to be her Arthur Miller, but she had no eyes for me. Later she became one of the dreaded informers who handed over Jews living in hiding to the clutches of the Gestapo. Clearly, like many spies, she was 'turned'. After the Gestapo had her in their power, she betrayed her own kind. Many people could be corrupted by threats and promises. Only a few could overcome their fear of death and use their wits, wiles and presence of mind to lead the enemy astray and avoid betraying anyone. Apart from her looks, Stella had no particular qualities. And probably the mere threat to smash in her beautiful teeth was enough to induce her to cooperate.

When I saw her in the distance coming along Ansbacher Strasse, my heart beat a bit faster. I had more to offer now than in those days at school. I had a foolproof passport, perfect accommodation, a sailing boat and money. And now my old flame from school was coming towards me. She smiled, and we went for a cup of tea in a café. She looked up at me. When I covered her hand with mine, next to the glass of tea, she did not withdraw it.

When I asked her 'Would you like to see my illegal room?', she didn't say no. Our tea, hardly touched, stood getting cold. And there we were on the rear platform of a tram to Kleiststrasse. Up ahead, a crowd of passengers was getting on. Suddenly Stella asked me: 'Are you sure you're not making a mistake?' 'Yes, you're right. Come on, let's get off again.'

Later she was given the task of catching me, the pass-forger Cioma Schönhaus alias Günther Rogoff. Her words about making a mistake had been a declaration of love. But what inner voice had made me say: 'You're right, let's get off'? The pea had been lucky.

I went to the KaDeWe (Kaufhaus des Westens) department store and bought another book about sailing, one for advanced learners this time, and a bottle of perfume for Dr

Meier's wife. Then I sauntered along Tauentzienstrasse to Bleibtreustrasse, my steps as light as a feather. Amazing what a new passport can do.

Dr Meier congratulated me on the document proving my White Russian identity. But I still wasn't quite satisfied, and asked him for a favour: 'You're still living in your flat and receiving post normally. I'd like to send you a letter addressed in pencil. Please keep the envelope, and when I come over I'll erase the address and replace it with the fictitious one that I gave to the White Russian bureau, No. 10 Meinekestrasse, Berlin. Then anybody finding the envelope in my wallet will be convinced that I really do live there. It will be one more piece of evidence to strengthen the credibility of my wallet.'

Moreover, in Turmstrasse there was one of those Berlin tobacco shops that ran lending libraries on the side. I went there, paid a small subscription, took out two books and was given a membership card allowing me to borrow books for the next six months. The card was made out in the name of Peter Petrov, born 7 July 1922. Another confirmation of my legitimacy.

When I showed my wallet to Dr Kaufmann, he said he thought nothing could happen to me now. 'That's just as well, Schönhaus, because we need you. *Fortune oblige*. There are big challenges ahead of us. The demand for passes in Berlin and throughout the Reich is increasing. I'm going to introduce you to my most important female assistant, another member of the Confessing Church. She needs your services. I've arranged for you to meet. Go along to the underground station at Breitenbachplatz at ten tomorrow morning. There'll be a young woman waiting for you by the big map of the city. Ask her for directions to Gefkenstrasse. That's the password. The rest you can arrange with her personally. Her name is Helene Jacobs.'

I was at the Breitenbachplatz punctually the next morning. The U-Bahn station was empty. A young woman was standing in front of the city map, and I went up to her. 'Can you tell me how to get to Gefkenstrasse?' She was petite, and as she walked her feet pointed outwards like a ballerina's. Her complexion was poor, and her blonde hair straggly. Her clothes were completely unfashionable. But she looked at me trustingly, with wide, intelligent eyes. She questioned me confidently. Then she took a bundle of passes out of her handbag: seven passes and a post-office ID card. Each had the appropriate photo clipped to it. Her movements were so unselfconscious and natural that no passer-by would have suspected there was anything illegal going on here. 'When can I have them back?' 'Tomorrow.' 'Good. Bring them to me. I live at No. 2 Bonner Strasse, fifth floor. If you come at two o'clock you can meet Pastor Kurt Müller from Stuttgart. He'll be taking the passes back with him.'

And so began my friendship with Helene Jacobs.

Pastor Kurt Müller was anything but what you would expect a pastor to be. He was tall and powerfully built, with the face of a seaman, and a pipe in the corner of his mouth. He greeted me in his bass voice, gave me a massive paw, and acted as though he'd known me for God knows how long. Then he took the passes over to a window, examined each one through the spectacles perched on the end of his nose, brought a fist down gently on the table, handed the papers on to Helene Jacobs, and said simply: 'I'll be back. There are so many more people in need of these.' When he went to leave, he put on his broad-brimmed hat and looked like a real pastor. The right kind.

Satisfied, I went back by tram to our shop in the Waldstrasse. Ludwig was out on the philatelic hunt again. I was alone.

The letter with the address in pencil arrived promptly at Dr

Meier's. I put it in my wallet with the new passport. If there was a police check, at least I wouldn't hear that nagging voice saying: 'You made that pass yourself . . . made it yourself . . . made it yourself.' Now it was authentic!

It was almost a physical pleasure. I went to look at my passport again. Where was it? I searched thoroughly. I turned out all my pockets. My wallet was gone! How could that have happened? Probably when I paid my fare in the tram I'd missed my inside jacket pocket putting it back, and it had fallen out between my shirt and trousers as I got off. On the tram? Or out in the street? There was no knowing.

But it hadn't necessarily gone straight to the police. It might have been found by somebody who needed identity papers himself. Or perhaps a child was playing with my wallet at that moment. I turned back the bedclothes and lay down fully dressed, in broad daylight, pulling the blanket over my head. Help me, dear God! What should I do now? 'Don't do anything. Just wait.'

If they found the envelope addressed to me and tried to return the wallet there, they'd find I was unknown at that address. Then they would look for me at AEG, but nobody knew me there either. Then the police would check on me at the lending library in Turmstrasse. And everywhere they would tell people the same thing: 'If Peter Petrov shows up, inform the police immediately!'

But still I bided my time, trying to reassure myself: 'Just calm down. You can phone the lending library by late afternoon, and you'll see from their reaction whether anyone's been checking up on you there.' Admittedly, that was highly unlikely, but just before six I went to a telephone box. With bated breath I dialled the number. Someone at the lending library responded. 'Excuse me, it's Peter Petrov speaking. I've lost my wallet. I think I may have left it at your shop. Have you come across it, by any chance?' I thought I wasn't hearing correctly. At the other end of the line the lending-library proprietor was saying: 'Yes, Herr Petrov, your wallet is here. When do you want to come and collect it?' I felt as though somebody was choking me. I couldn't utter a word, and silently I put the receiver down. The worst that could happen had happened.

I hadn't been to the lending library for weeks.

I paced to and fro, to and fro in the shop, like a caged monkey. The worst thing was that I had brought about my own downfall. Mama always said: 'He'd be a nice boy if only he could be a bit more organized.' Now she was gone. Papa as well. I needed him. On Sundays our neighbours always used to come and consult him on all sorts of questions. Where was he now?

I had only one last indirect link with him here on earth. His last friend, to whom he had given his bread ration when he was leaving prison: Werner Schlesinger. He was still around! And I knew where to find him: in Steglitz. In Schloss Strasse, on the corner of Markelstrasse. There was a restaurant there that served game dishes without ration coupons. I had met him there before in the evening. I hoped he would be eating there, so that I could tell him what had happened. Perhaps he would know what to do.

Since the police had already enquired at the lending library, they were obviously taking the hunt for Peter Petrov seriously. And because I had probably lost my wallet somewhere between the tram stop and our shop, they would be looking for me in this district. I would have to be careful. To disguise myself slightly, I borrowed Ludwig's hat, without waiting for permission. I pulled it down over my face. A glance in the mirror, and then I was off to Steglitz.

The restaurant in Steglitz consisted of two large, long rooms. As you entered, the nickel-topped counter of the beer bar was on your right. On the left were small, round-topped

marble tables with cast-iron legs, seating about forty customers. Beyond them were two large double doors leading to
the rear of the restaurant, where there was room for another
fifty people at identical marble tables.

Behind the double door on the right sat Ruth Schlesinger,
Werner's wife. There was also a stranger sitting at her table. He
was eating meat and spinach. I joined them, shook hands with
Ruth, and ordered a beer. For the moment I said nothing, so
that I wouldn't have to repeat my story later; I preferred to wait
for Werner. I hung Ludwig's hat on a hook immediately above
my head, and my briefcase containing Frau Schirrmacher's keys
below it. Then I lit a cigarette.

Ruth asked me to stand up to let her out. She needed to go
to the toilet. As she squeezed past me, I saw Werner
Schlesinger coming. 'There's Werner,' I said, and Ruth dashed
forward to tell him off: 'Why do you always come so late,
when you know how much it worries me?' Werner put his
finger to his mouth, winked and hissed: 'Police!'

Almost every seat in the place was occupied. I was still
standing, and I now took a step to the right, towards the next
table. As casually as possible, I asked: 'Could I take a look at
your menu, please?' Glasses were clinking, people laughing.
Behind me I heard: 'But the beer is still there; the cigarette is
still there.'

I went to the next table: 'Could I have a look at your
menu, please?' I could see the backs of the two figures. The
sound drummed in my ears: 'But the cigarette's still there.
And so is the beer.' Quite slowly I went on to the next table:
'Can I see your menu, please?' Then I stopped. Another three
steps forward: 'Can I look at your menu, please?' The high
noise level protected me like a wall. 'Can I see your menu,
please?' I stopped again, and made out that I was reading. I
moved very slowly. Another three steps to the double doors.
At the next table: 'Can I have a look at your menu, please?'

I could already hear the noise from the street. As an extra precaution, I stopped once more. 'Could I have a look at your menu, please?'

And then I moved, as though in slow motion, as far as the exit, and with measured tread down the three steps to the pavement. Once out on the street, I still strolled, as though taking a boring walk. I sauntered round the corner. But then I pelted away like a bull escaping slaughter. I raced along Markelstrasse as far as the Südwestkorso. My footsteps echoed on the pavement. They slowed down at the Hohenzollerndamm and then along Auguste-Viktoria-Strasse. At last I stood outside No. 92 Paulsborner Strasse, the building where Tatjana lived.

Jankowski opened the door: 'Tatjana, come here. Cioma's alive!' Jankowski kissed me like a brother, Russian-style. I wiped his tears from my face. 'Cioma, I was so worried about you. You've got no idea what went on in our office today. A Superintendent Wulkow is conducting the investigation. They're assuming that a Russian spy – perhaps even a parachutist – has been trying to mingle with the accredited White Russians. Taboritzki is running around with a bright red face, constantly muttering: "I just can't understand it." But the Superintendent is certain they'll soon catch the spy, because from tomorrow a poster with your photo will be displayed in every police station in the Reich. A picture of you is also going to appear in the next "Special Edition of the *German Police Gazette*". You can't show your face in public, Cioma.'

'But if they're starting to put out my photo in police stations today, Herr Jankowski, then I've still got another three days before all the policemen begin to recognize me in the street. I'm going to sleep in my room at Frau Schirrmacher's again tonight. That's where I feel safest. Tomorrow I'll phone Dr Kaufmann, and take it from there.' Tatjana did not agree.

Because my keys were in my briefcase, and the briefcase was hanging on a rack underneath Ludwig's hat in the restaurant in Markelstrasse, I had to ring the doorbell at Frau Schirrmacher's. 'Hello, where are your keys, Herr Schönhausen?' 'Oh, Frau Schirrmacher, I've done something stupid. I left my briefcase on the tram, with the keys in it.' Frau Schirrmacher smiled. 'Schönhausen, Schönhausen, what are we to do with you? But it doesn't matter that you've lost your keys. You won't even have to go to the lost property office.' She went into her room, opened a drawer, and gave me some replacement keys. 'Do you see this little number at the top? We have my late husband to thank for this – the number is registered with the police. If the keys are handed in at the lost property office, the police will automatically bring them back to me. So you see, it's no great misfortune.'

'But Frau Schirrmacher, there's something else I haven't had a chance to tell you yet. When I went home today I found there was a registered letter from district military headquarters. I've got to present myself at Lichterfelde Barracks tomorrow morning. I want to sleep at home on my last night, so I'll have to say goodbye to you now, this very evening.' 'That's what I've feared all along, Schönhausen. But that is the fate of all young German men when the Fatherland is in danger.'

Trekking with my suitcase through the pitch-black streets, I found my way to the Waldstrasse without any trouble. Though I did nearly bang my head on a post box, the darkness was an advantage; I valued the protection of the blackout, because a young man moving through the streets at night with a suitcase invited checks. And I no longer had ID papers of any kind.

In the middle of the night I knocked seven times, as agreed, on the door of our shop in Waldstrasse. 'Schönhaus? What's wrong? Have you gone mad? Do you know the time?' 'Yes,

Ludwig, give me a chance to explain.' After I'd told him about my lucky escape, Ludwig only asked: 'So where's my hat?'

Next morning I went to Dr Kaufmann. 'Schönhaus,' he said, after I had described my disaster to him, 'I too have a confession to make: I never quite believed your story about the burnt passes. But now I see how carelessly you treat your own passport, I believe you.' 'Thanks, Herr Doktor. It just shows that everything has its positive side, however bad things are.' 'All right, there are two things I'm going to do straight away, Schönhaus. I've still got my old connections with Minister Popitz.[38] He'll find out for me from the police authorities whether the hunt for you is as intensive as Herr Jankowski claims.'

I stood by while he phoned. It took him almost half an hour to make the connection, and as long again before the return call came. 'Wanted posters about a certain Peter Petrov have been circulated? Yes? Really? Highest alert, indeed? And throughout the Reich? Thank you, Herr Popitz.' Kaufmann replaced the receiver and looked at me sadly. 'Yes, my dear chap. It's looking bad. You really won't be able to show your face in public. Right: the next thing is we need somewhere for you to stay.' He did some more phoning. But nobody was prepared to take on a young man who was wanted throughout the Reich.

'We'll try Helene Jacobs next. You already know her.' 'Yes,' she said on the telephone, 'I'll take him. We need him for our work.' Dr Kaufmann was relieved. 'You can depend on that young woman. Now we'll have to work out how you can get there.' 'I'll have to go back just once more to the Waldstrasse. I've left my eyelet punch there, and I need it for fixing the photos into passes. I could pick up my box of watercolours with the Japanese brushes, too. It's only just before noon; it can't be that dangerous yet.'

Helene Jacobs

The terminus of bus route No. 11 lay diagonally opposite the shop in the Waldstrasse. It was about thirty metres away. The bus was empty. The driver and conductor stood in front of it chatting. Apart from them, nobody was around, and there were only a few pedestrians to be seen in the whole street. Nobody got on the bus. As it happened, Ludwig wanted to go to Olivaer Platz, which was on the way to Bonner Strasse, where Helene lived. Everything looked quiet, so he came along, although maintaining a distance of ten paces behind me. It was a double-decker bus, and we went up to the top deck. I went first, and then Ludwig followed me after an interval. It was empty upstairs, as well. I sat down on the front bench, on the far right. The seat was wide, with room for eight passengers. Ludwig sat on the far left. The bus slowly filled up, and after about ten minutes it set off.

My brown leather bag had a shoulder strap. I kept hold of it, so that the bag wouldn't slide away from me when we cornered. After the fifth stop I had the sensation of something glittering behind me. I turned round. Three seats behind me sat a man, about fifty years old, with a bald, tanned head, wearing a dark blue suit with a waistcoat. His jacket was open, and a gold watch chain was dangling from his waistcoat pocket. That was what was glittering. As I was looking at the man, he got up and changed his seat. Now he was sitting right behind me. He rested both arms on my seat back and asked: 'Is that your bag there?' As naturally as possible, I forced myself to say: 'Yes, so what? What's it got to do with you?' He replied: 'Take it easy, my lad. Calm down.' 'What is it you want?' I asked indignantly. But baldhead refused to be intimidated. He seemed to be thinking hard. Then he turned to the left and asked Ludwig: 'Are you together?' White as a sheet, Ludwig denied it. 'And where are you going?' 'To Olivaer Platz.'

And again I watched the man as he thought, and thought, and thought. I tried the indignant passenger act again, but the effect was becoming weaker all the time. The man just repeated: 'Just you stay calm. Take it easy.' Thoughts were whirling through my head. 'It's all over now. You'll never get out of this.' My only comfort was a black silk tie. I carried it folded in my back trouser pocket, just in case. With any luck, I could hang myself with it before they started to torture me. Baldhead sat motionless behind us. The bus travelled from stop to stop. The conductor called out, 'Olivaer Platz.' Ludwig stood up and went to the stairs. The man followed him, paused for a moment, looked at me penetratingly, and then he too went down the stairs.

I tried to grasp what was going on here. Baldhead must be a seasoned police officer due to retire soon. Now, at his ripe age, he had been lucky enough to come across a wanted criminal. He was wondering what to do. According to regulations, he should have arrested me. But not before following me to see who else I could lead him to.

Out of sheer excitement he had already partly given himself away. But he could still pursue me. I would have to get off somewhere, and then he would follow me. So he would have taken up his position on the platform below, behind the stairs, where he could wait unseen to follow me. If my supposition was right, there was only one thing to do: fasten my leather bag around me, slide down the stairs silently with both arms on the handrails, and jump off the bus while it was still moving. At school, I was always pretty good at the thousand-metre race. I had the advantage of youth, and I'd always enjoyed jumping off moving buses.

We were approaching Bonner Strasse. At a bend the bus turned into the Südwestkorso, and the driver slowed down. I glided slowly, both elbows on the rails, down the stairs; very quietly, so that nothing was audible from below. Then I jumped. Fortunately, I didn't fall over. Fortunately, the bus did not stop. Fortunately, there was no detective chasing me.

I raced down one street to the left, and then another to the right, then I darted off down another side street, and into the entrance to a building. I let down the paper blackout blind there and made a little hole in it with my finger to see if anyone was coming. No, nobody. I waited a while. Then I walked slowly to No. 2 Bonner Strasse. On the fifth floor there was a door marked HELENE JACOBS on a gold background. For me it was real gold. Helene let me in, and we sat in her kitchen. I was finding out how exciting life could be. Sometimes a little too exciting.

I had not yet finished my account – of how I acquired my genuine White Russian passport – when there was a ring at the door. It was Ludwig. 'What did baldy do? Did he stay on the platform downstairs, or did he follow you to Olivaer Platz?' 'No, no. He stayed on the bus. He was probably waiting for Peter Petrov . . .'

Helene made tea and served the last slices of her home-made strudel. We all sat on kitchen stools. 'You don't need to worry any more, Schönhaus. Nobody will come for you here. You can stay here until the war is over. You've brought your pass-forging tools with you, so we can get down to work again soon. We'll share the work: I collect the passes from Kaufmann, you work on them, and I distribute them.' Ludwig was getting restless. He wanted to go to his stamp dealers. He decided that the business on the bus was nothing out of the ordinary.

Ludwig was kind enough, but rather a dour character. After all we had been through together, it never occurred to him (as the older of us two) to offer to call me by the familiar 'Du' form of address. Yet he was a genuinely decent and reliable man. It was completely different with Helene; as soon as Ludwig was gone, she held out her hand and said: 'Just call me Helene.'

She was employed by a lawyer specializing in patents. She was working her way through her education, and had taken her school-leaving exams under a special arrangement for gifted students. Her father had been the headmaster of a grammar school in Schneidemühl, who had lost his job in circumstances similar to Professor Unrath's in the film *The Blue Angel*. At an early age, Helene had to provide for herself and her family. She had previously worked for a Jewish specialist in patent law, very patriotically minded, who had not the least intention of leaving his homeland. Helene eventually persuaded him to emigrate to America. He was probably the first person whose life she ever saved.

Her appearance had the effect of making her almost invisible. At first sight she looked like an innocent from the country, and she was clever at using this disguise.

When the first Berlin Jews were deported to the extermination camps, some managed to send postcards asking for food. Helene sent them parcels of groceries. She was then summoned by the Gestapo. The official looked at her in astonishment: 'Tell me, have you taken leave of your senses? Sending food parcels to the Jews in the east? Giving your full address? What on earth were you thinking of?' Helene replied: 'Just a moment. Think about it. You are a German man and I am a German woman. These people are starving, and I send them something to eat. From a human point of view, do you find that reprehensible?' The official reflected: 'Well, I can understand it from a human point of view. But not from a National Socialist one!' 'Hold on,' said Helene, and went on to ask: 'So you distinguish between a human standpoint and a National Socialist one?' Whereupon he roared at her: 'Just get out of here!'

And she got away with it. That was Helene Jacobs.

Helene's flat was actually nothing short of a library. While she was away at work during the day I had time to read and think. Ludwig dropped in now and again – disguised as a plumber. He always carried a big bag of tools draped around him, and wore a peaked cap and blue overalls. We played chess or listened to the BBC, which Germans were strictly forbidden to do. If you got caught, you risked being sent to a concentration camp. The BBC call sign was a real give-away: boom-boom-boom-*booom*, boom-boom-boom-*booom*.[39] You had to turn the radio down very low, because that call sign could be heard right through doors and walls. We heard reports of what was happening to the Jews in Poland. The horror seeped like a fog into peaceful No. 2 Bonner Strasse.

Regularly, every morning, Aunt Lieschen brought some provisions. She was Helene's eighty-year-old aunt. My job was to cook something tasty for dinner. After supper Helene and I would talk, over a glass of wine. Neither of us was willing simply to accept the situation we found ourselves in. We agreed on one idea: in our diminishingly small world the kind of original Christianity that Leo Tolstoy wrote about should be compulsory for the whole of humanity. And once there was no longer any distinction between Christians and Jews, anti-Semitism would automatically vanish. We developed a world view that united us, and out of it grew an unshakeable friendship.

This was the wartime year of 1943. Summer slowly came. Life in Helene's flat became routine. In the morning Aunt Lieschen arrived with fresh bread. I made tea. Helene took some sandwiches and went off to work. Aunt Lieschen cleared up. Then it was quiet. I was alone.

In front of me I had twenty-three post-office ID cards and fourteen passes. I completed the stamps and stuck in the new owners' photographs. In German, the eagle with its swastika was literally the 'eagle of sovereignty' (*Hoheitsadler*), the emblem of state power: it was fun to deprive it of its sovereignty. Against its will, it would now be helping Jews living in hiding to avoid arrest. The more stamps I forged, the more adept I became at it. Thanks to BBC broadcasts, the news trickling out about the treatment of Jews in Poland became ever clearer. Over there, atrocities; back here, sun shining into the room. And the only sound was the ticking of the clock on the wall.

My thoughts were in Poland. What was it like to live in such a camp? Would you have a toothbrush there? Was there toilet paper? How did you sleep at night? Were there wooden bunks? Were there straw mattresses? My vision of white huts was surely wrong. Where was Mama now? What had she been forced to see? What had they done to her? Where had Papa been when he wrote the postcard? The postcard that said: 'I've been looking for Mama everywhere. Cioma was right about everything. I'm glad he's not here with us. Farewell.' I had treasured this card like a holy relic. Trustingly, I gave it to Tatjana for safekeeping. She stuck it to the underside of her cupboard, but when she heard they were looking for me, she became scared and burned it. I took that very hard. Writing a postcard in Majdanek was a mighty feat for Papa to perform, as well as organizing a postage stamp, and ensuring that the card actually arrived. Now the card was gone – so everything was gone.

But Helene's flat, on the fifth floor at No. 2 Bonner Strasse, was there. That was reality. I lay in a deckchair on the sunny terrace and let my dreams rise into the blue sky. Sparrows twittered, pigeons cooed. There was only a faint noise of traffic coming up from the street. Only a few cars were moving, and they were fuelled by wood burners. Petrol was reserved for the *Wehrmacht*.

Among many books in the flat, I discovered Heinrich Heine's *Disputation*. That evening I declaimed the fourteen-page poem to Helene. There was a duel of words between a rabbi and a Capuchin monk, in front of the assembled Spanish court. At the end, the King asked his Queen: 'Tell me, what is your opinion? Which of these is right, forsooth? Which of this pair, by your reckoning, is the owner of the truth?' Donna Blanka looked at him, pressed her clenched fists to her brow, thought long and hard, and finally spoke: 'Who is right, I cannot tell. But I know well that methinks the monk is smelly, by my troth, and the rabbi also stinks.' We laughed. He was a cheeky character, this Heine. But somehow he was right. We agreed on that.

The rise and fall of air-raid warning sirens dragged us back to reality. 'What are we going to do now? You can't come down to the air-raid shelter, Cioma, because you don't officially live in my flat. So I'm going to stay up here as well. And if we're hit by a bomb, then that's it – we'll die together.' After ten minutes, there was a ring at the door. It was the air-raid warden: 'Fräulein Jacobs, why aren't you in the shelter?' Helene's reply was quick-witted: 'Oh, come on, the British always miss.' But he came back with: 'Don't argue – just follow orders.' And they went downstairs together.

When Ludwig came next morning, we arranged for him to bring me the spare pieces of rope from my locker in the boathouse. Ludwig, ever the man of action, appeared the same afternoon, heavily laden. We attached one rope end to the central heating radiator, and stowed the line made from all the other joined-up pieces under the radiator. If a bomb ever did fall, but only destroyed the well of the staircase, I could let myself down the front of the building by the rope. Fortunately, this life-saving arrangement was never put to the test.

But lives were constantly saved at No. 2 Bonner Strasse, without the need for ropes or nets. Helene's flat was a meeting point for members of the Confessing Church who risked their lives to save Jews.

The Friday deadline for deliveries still applied, even in Bonner Strasse. The only difference was that, instead of my going to Dr Kaufmann, he came to me. The weighty newspaper *Das Reich* might have been specially designed for carrying my weekly output of thirty-seven passes. One Friday, he brought a newspaper full of ID cards with him as usual. But that day, he suddenly stopped short, looking at Helene, then at me, and then back at Helene. He wagged a forefinger: 'Schönhaus, Schönhaus, what have you done to our little Helene? I wouldn't have recognized her. Look at that perfect complexion, those flowing locks, those radiant eyes. It's obvious the prince has kissed a frog and turned it into a princess.'

Helene turned away. She went out to the hall and opened the door to Ludwig. Without a word of greeting he flew to the radio and switched it on. 'Listen to this, all of you!' The Führer was speaking: 'The defection of Italy means very little, because for months it has been German forces above all that have carried and sustained the fight in that country. We are now free of irksome constraints.' Ludwig was excited: 'Did you get that? Italy has surrendered.' Dr Kaufmann smiled quietly: 'I've known about it since yesterday. And a good deal more. My children, you can't imagine what's building up behind the scenes in the highest *Wehrmacht* circles. I think we could be celebrating the end of the war before the year is out. A change of mood is taking place at the top which the Führer will not survive. A former officer and chief secretary like me could never have dreamt that things would get to such a pitch in our Fatherland. However, whatever is happening, Schönhaus, you've got to keep your head down. The authorities still have your "wanted" poster pinned up everywhere. Don't move an inch outside until it's all over.'

Helene was not in the mood to be lectured at, even indirectly, and she shot back with: 'You can rely on me to make sure Schönhaus stays here. But what about your notebook with the addresses and phone numbers of all the Jews in hiding? What happens if you're arrested? You would endanger everybody who has placed his trust in you.' 'You're right, Helene. But I'll make sure in good time that my notebook is safe, whenever I hear from Minister Popitz that they've got something on me and I'm a wanted man. For the moment, thank God, that is not the case.'

Boldness doesn't always pay

Hailstones rattled against the window panes. The sky was dark. A balcony door slammed shut. Lightning lit up the living room, followed by a clap of thunder like a falling bomb. Ludwig and Helene reached the building just in time. He took off his peaked cap and shook it out, spattering the mirror from top to bottom in the process. 'Hey, you're not by yourself in your workshop now!' 'I'm sorry, Fräulein Jacobs. I'll clean the mirror up straight away. And by the way, I'm not alone in my workshop any more. The third musketeer, Werner Scharff, moved in yesterday. He's got a real tale to tell, believe me. He was chief electrician in the Jewish congregation building that the Gestapo took over. Almost all the officials there knew him. Despite telling him he was safe, they made him train up an Aryan electrician. And then one day, still in his work clothes, they rushed him headlong on to the next transport. He didn't come to his senses until he was already in the goods wagon. The first thing he did was feel along the seam of his trousers. He was in luck: the metal-saw blades were still there.

'The moment the train moved, he slipped over to the corner where the ventilation flap was, climbed up on the edges of the slop bucket, and started sawing at the hinges. He had wound insulating tape round one end of the saw blade, as a wise precaution, so that he could keep on sawing without so much effort or pain. He only stopped when somebody needed to use the bucket. And a lot of people did, just to obstruct him. Most of them pleaded with him to stop, because they were afraid that if he escaped they would all be shot.

'Meanwhile, the train had come to a halt, and stood for ages in the sun. Finally, after much tireless sawing, the ventilation flap came away; the train travelled on slowly and stopped once more for quite a long time in the Spreewald forest. When it was growing dark, Werner Scharff dropped out through the hatch. It was a heavy fall, but he didn't break anything. The guards were obviously asleep. He rolled down the embankment, landed on the high road to Berlin, and moved off. In the evening he went to a village inn and ordered a complete meal, but in the middle of the last course he went to the lavatory and disappeared into the darkness. This morning he knocked seven times at the shop door. I thought it must be Schönhaus, but it was him.'

Helene and I were fascinated by the story, and invited Ludwig to stay for supper. But he was going into town, despite the blackout. He had an appointment with an old school friend who worked in the district military office. That was where those two blank service passbooks had come from. Long before, when I had first met Ludwig at Dr Meier's, I had promised to fill them both in. At that time it would have been something of a luxury, but now it was a matter of life or death, particularly for me. But I still needed someone with a *Wehrmacht* passbook I could use as a model. I couldn't produce the right stamps without a template to work from.

There was a kind of peacetime quality about life at Helene's. It was all very regular. Gertrud Staewen came on one occasion, and Etta von Oertzen stayed for a few days.[40] Pastor Müller came over from Stuttgart now and again: he was a pupil of Karl Barth's.[41] There were some interesting conversations. He told us that Pastor Martin Niemöller[42] always used to open his service on Sunday with the words: 'All right, now that the gentlemen of the Gestapo have joined us, let us pray in God's name.' Pastor Niemöller was in a concentration camp by then. But his congregation made sure that I never ran out of work.

It was by no means a foregone conclusion that the eighty-year-old Aunt Lieschen would accept me. Passport forgery was a serious crime in Germany, punishable by death. Anybody sheltering Jews or helping them in any way might end up in prison or a concentration camp. The Jacobs family regarded Helene as a security risk, and for that reason her sister-in-law Edeltraut no longer contacted her. But Helene was not to be deterred from her activities.

Before 1933 Helene had almost been engaged. He was a head taller than her, but equally blond and blue-eyed. However, that was all they had in common. He was convinced that only the strong hand of the Führer could save Germany from ruin. 'Only when our National Socialist youth are cured of this feeble Christian idea of loving thy neighbour, only when they learn to develop the ferocity of a predator will they succeed in vanquishing our enemies.' These were the words he used to explain the world to her. But Helene, on the other hand, felt that 'A government that makes a virtue out of cruelty and a weakness out of Christian love for others, endangers our Fatherland. Destructiveness always turns upon itself eventually.'

Helene described how, in the election year before Hitler's 'seizure of power', she and her friends from the Centre Party formed a chain, walking along arm-in-arm down Potsdamer Strasse chanting: 'Long live our much-loved Heinrich Brüning!'[43] The political mood at the time had been extremely tense. When Helene arrived home that evening, there was an SA man at the door. Brown uniform, high black boots, and a swastika armband. She was afraid she was about to be arrested for her anti-Nazi attitude. But it was much worse than that. The man at the door wanted to impress her with his uniform. It was her boyfriend. The engagement was off.

Betrayed

On Friday Dr Kaufmann brought me more of the passes that had been dropped into their collecting box by the Dahlem congregation. He looked anxious. His housekeeper had warned him: 'Two gentlemen from the Gestapo have been here asking for you.' Although he had been informed by Minister Popitz, apparently reliably, that he was not wanted for anything, all the same – to be on the safe side – he was keen to retrieve the passes from the sewing basket under his bookcase. We warned him against it, but one of his assistants, called Hallermann,[44] offered to get the passes. He wanted to play the hero at all costs; he was always trying to prove himself. He proposed to climb up the side of the house at night, break in through the window, and redeem the incriminating material.

The telephone rang the next afternoon, and Helene took the call. Hallermann wanted to know where he could meet Dr Kaufmann. Helene said she didn't know. He then said he wanted to meet Helene at Feuerbachstrasse station. It was urgent.

She went. From the balcony, I watched her leave. Then I waited. It got dark, and I prepared a supper – apple pancakes. The wall clock struck ten, then eleven and twelve. The ticking of the clock told me something terrible had happened. It was important to stay calm and collected. I started to tidy up the flat: I put everything that might incriminate Helene into a large briefcase. She must surely have been arrested. The next thing they would do was search the flat. I had to disappear, because my presence would incriminate her.

I was at the bus stop by five in the morning, when the first buses started running. The police would not be up so early. My 'wanted' poster was a couple of months old by then, and even if it wasn't yellowing yet – so what. I had to get to Ludwig's in the Waldstrasse; I had no other choice. On the bus it occurred to me that I had left two important things behind in Helene's flat: the eyelet-punch, and a briefcase full of hundred-mark notes. Some elements at the top of German society were happy to donate large sums to rescue Jews. Anonymously, of course. The money was intended for a Gestapo man called Freudenberg, who claimed that he could save Jews from the gas chamber. He wanted a thousand marks per head.

The case of money and the eyelet-punch absolutely had to be retrieved from the flat.

Ludwig listened. He sat on the sofa with his head buried in his hands. 'It was bound to happen sooner or later. It's amazing she hasn't been arrested before now. And as for you, Schönhaus, you're not putting your nose outside the door again. Think of what happened on the bus.' 'Ludwig, I'm not the only one the police are looking for. And it's two months ago now. There'll be a whole new crop of "wanted" posters on the police station notice boards by now. I absolutely must go back just once more to Bonner Strasse. Stupidly, I left the eyelet-punch there. And a big briefcase full of hundred-mark notes. It's money that Dr Kaufmann collected because a corrupt Gestapo official claimed to be able to bring Jews back to Theresienstadt, where "their survival was guaranteed". What can Helene say when the Gestapo ask her who this forger's eyelet-punch belongs to and where she got all that money?'

'Don't go to the flat, Schönhaus. You'll only put Fräulein Jacobs in even greater danger. The police are bound to be there searching the place. And one of them is certain to be waiting by the telephone to see who calls.' 'Don't worry, Ludwig. It's simple: before I go into the flat, I'll phone from the box on the corner. Then it will be safe to go in.' 'If you ask me, simple is what *you* are, Schönhaus!'

I went back to Bonner Strasse by bus. The journey was still unnerving for me. The detective with the bald head and the gold watch-chain was still so vivid in my memory that I stayed on the platform downstairs, ready to jump off if need be. It would be better still if I had a new bike. The old one my cousin had left me was scrap metal by now. With a new bike I could not be followed so easily. If my cobbler in Dragonerstrasse could provide me with an eyelet-punch, then he could supply a bicycle as well. We would see.

I got off at the corner of the Südwestkorso and Bonner Strasse. The entrance was visible from the telephone box. I let Helene's phone ring ten times. Nobody picked up the receiver. So there was nobody there. Up I went! Leaving the door open so that I would hear if anybody came up the stairs, I stowed the two *corpora delicti* away. But before I left, I sat at the table for a minute. The apple pancakes were still there. Inwardly, I said goodbye to our little paradise.

On the way back to the Waldstrasse my eye was caught by a gleaming barber's shop sign. That was what I needed. 'A military cut, please. By this time tomorrow I'll be in the army.' The barber laughed. 'At least you've got something worth cutting. It's a long time since you last saw a barber.' With my new short-back-and-sides, the feeling of being a hunted man was swept away on the wind.

The bicycle

The cobbler looked at me over his glasses: 'So, we want to buy a bike, do we? They don't exist any more, neither new nor second-hand.' 'And what if I'm prepared to pay two or three thousand marks for one?' 'Hang on, did I hear right? You can pay three thousand marks? Come back tomorrow afternoon. I'll have one for you by then.'

And what a bike it turned out to be: balloon tyres, comfortable saddle, wide luggage carrier, and a chrome headlamp with a dynamo. The size of my fortune had shrunk, but a plan was taking shape in my mind. I bowled along Unter den Linden as though I was flying. In front of the Adlon Hotel a horseshoe was lying on the ground. Only a small one, from the heel of a military boot. I picked it up, nonetheless.

Ludwig confirmed that cycling was safer than using buses or trams. With the briefcase on the luggage carrier, I went straight on to visit Etta von Oertzen. She greeted me outside in her garden, behind a hazelnut bush. 'Come over here, if you don't mind. You know, because of the neighbours. You are a wanted man, after all. Let's sit on this bench.' She looked around. 'I've got something important to tell you. I had a phone call from Helene yesterday, even though she was arrested the day before. They put her in the Bessemer Strasse prison. Yesterday some bombs fell on it, and the walls collapsed. The prison authorities had no option but to send the prisoners home, on condition that they returned the next day. Helene spent the night with Aunt Lieschen. Lots of her friends or acquaintances would have sheltered her but, so as not worry Aunt Lieschen, she chose to go back to prison early next morning. She sends her love, and says you must take care. There is an intensive hunt going on for you.'

We both fell silent. There were no words for Helene's heroic action.

It was only after the war that I found out what had happened. Helene Jacobs was arrested on 17 August 1943, and on 11 January 1944 she was sentenced by Special Court III of the Berlin regional court to two and a half years' imprisonment for crimes against the war economy regulations, and for aiding and abetting the falsification of documents. Neither during interrogation nor during the trial did she incriminate or betray anyone. Helene acquitted herself so well that even the Nazi authorities were impressed. That was why the prison governor suggested to her one day: 'Fräulein Jacobs, if I can arrange a pardon for you, would you be willing to work for me in the prison office?' Helene agreed.

The chief warder with her big bunch of keys was astonished when the governor told her: 'This is no longer Prisoner Jacobs, but Fräulein Jacobs. She'll be working in the office from now on.' Shaking her head, the officer said: 'Strange way to run a prison – and getting stranger all the time.'

One day the governor warned Helene: 'It's time to clear off. The Russians are coming. I'm going to disappear. How about you?' 'No,' said Helene. 'Somebody's got to make sure the prisoners are fed.' And so she stayed on. In April 1945, in an orderly fashion, she closed the prison down. She gave every prisoner a certificate of discharge, important for gaining entitlement to ration cards. She supplied deserters with civilian clothes so that they did not end up as prisoners of war. And when the Russians arrived, Helene carried out an orderly handover of the whole prison complex to them. Then she walked off, through streets where Germans and Russians were still fighting. Nothing happened to her. She wanted to get back to Aunt Lieschen, who was suffering from tuberculosis. Helene nursed her for the next two years. Afterwards, she declined to participate in the West German economic miracle: she felt that the proper role for her was working for the compensation of victims.[45]

'And here is a briefcase full of money that was left behind in Bonner Strasse,' I told Frau von Oertzen. 'As you know, it was collected to pay the corrupt Gestapo official who claimed to rescue Jews.' Etta von Oertzen held out her hand to me. 'All the best: I hope you make it.' It would have been an imposition to ask her to let me stay with her. I had to get away from Berlin, out of reach, to Switzerland, to stop putting people at risk.

When I mentioned Switzerland, Ludwig tapped his forehead disparagingly: 'So, now we're heading for Switzerland, are we! Couldn't think of anything easier, I suppose? Tell me the name of a single person who's ever managed it. How are you going to pull it off? Without a local guide or a map, on your bike, just on the off-chance? If you ask me, Schönhaus, it would be easier to put a bullet in your head straight away. You can borrow my revolver if you like.' 'No thanks, Ludwig. You know what the Berliners say: "Never rush to meet your fate – Heaven is prepared to wait." Give me a chance to try out my plan. First things first. And the first thing is the bike: I've got that. The next step is our army passbooks.'

A long farewell to Berlin

I cycled past the Victory Column, a monument commemorating the German victory over the French in 1870/71. For me it commemorated my parents, because of a photograph showing them standing in front of it. Mama was highly pregnant with me when the photo was taken. The Kaiser's Berlin reminded them of Russian palaces, but they both loved Berlin more than their Russian homeland, because they enjoyed equality there, before the Nazi nightmare darkened the world.

I knew the city like the back of my hand. The bike sailed along. The balloon tyres cushioned me, and the saddle was made for relaxing on. A sense of freedom wafted around me like a cool breeze. I cycled along Charlottenstrasse, past Lutter & Wegener's wine tavern. It was there, over a century before, that the poet E.T.A. Hoffmann and the actor Ludwig Devrient had told their tall tales while paying homage to the god of wine. Dorothee and I had drunk a glass of wine in the historic tavern before watching a performance of Goethe's *Faust*.

On the Gendarmenmarkt, I noticed that a shop diagonally opposite the Prussian State Theatre had maps in the window. I left my bike by the door and went in. The salesman was up a ladder, while a long queue of customers waited at the counter. The ladder was leaning against a big cabinet with a great many numbered drawers. Three large maps of Germany hung on the wall, marked out with grids and reference numbers: on one of them it said 1:25,000, and on the others 1:50,000 and 1:100,000 respectively.

The people in the queue found the numbers of the maps they wanted, and when it was their turn they shouted them out to the man on the ladder. He called back: 'Got it, got it, got it.' Then they collected their maps, and paid at the till. That was all. It was my turn. I shouted out all the numbers on the General Staff maps covering the Swiss border, on a scale of 1:25,000. This seemed to present no problem, so I asked for maps showing the roads between Berlin and the Swiss border; scale of 1:100,000. As before, there was a cry from above: 'Got it, got it, got it.'

I strapped the thick parcel of maps to the luggage carrier, and left. Pedalling off, I felt like the rider in 'The Ride across Lake Constance'.[46]

I glided along past Sophienstrasse, where my parents used to live when the world was still in order. Nearby, in Kleine Hamburger Strasse, there used to be a junk shop where you could get army surplus gear. It was still there. I bought a fur-covered military knapsack of the kind that the Hitler Youth used for their excursions. In a bookshop, I acquired an item of Nazi literature, by way of an accessory: Joseph Goebbels' *Vom Kaiserhof zur Reichskanzlei* (From the Kaiserhof to the Reich Chancellery). If a suspicious policeman searched my luggage while I was on the road, he would have to concede that 'this lad is politically reliable'.

Ludwig was dumbfounded when he saw the maps. 'Now even I am beginning to believe you'll pull it off. Particularly as I've found someone with an army passbook that you could copy.' 'That's fantastic, Ludwig! How did you manage that?' 'Don't get too excited just yet. Go and see the man first. He's called Claus Schiff, and he lives in Adolf Hitler Platz.'

Claus Schiff was willing to let me use his service passbook as a template to work from. Only in his flat, however; he wouldn't let it leave the premises. But he didn't mind me working from morning to night for a whole week there, even when he was not at home. He created a space by a large window for me, and there I sat, with eighteen stamps to copy, twice over!

Claus Schiff was a 'half-breed' and had therefore been discharged from the military. He worked as a technical draughtsman. His profession alone made him an ideal model to copy; and furthermore he was an exceptionally decent type.

I arrived every morning at ten to eight, and he turned his flat over to me. He trusted me, even though he hardly knew me. I worked without interruption on the stamps in the service passbooks. My long practice stood me in good stead. After a week I showed my host the two grey booklets with the big sovereign eagle on the title page. Claus Schiff whistled through his teeth. 'All you need now,' he said, 'is somebody to fill in the information for you in the two passbooks. You can hardly do that yourself. I'll fill them in, if you like.' 'Certainly,' I said. Nonchalantly, he began to enter a name:

Hans Brück, born 7 July 1922. (It was easy to remember two sevens.) But I was horrified as I watched him at work.

It was well known that you couldn't pass muster as a *Wehrmacht* clerk unless you had copperplate-neat handwriting. But Claus Schiff was just scribbling away, rapidly and casually. It was too late to stop him. What could I do? The script had to be the same throughout the document. It's ruined, I thought. However, I was too polite to let it show; he meant well, so I simply thanked him. But I filled in the second passbook myself, the one intended for Ludwig.

Both passbooks lay on my little desk in our shop. Ludwig reassured me about Claus Schiff's scrawl. But then came the acid test. Ludwig took them to his friend at district military headquarters. 'Have a good look at these two passbooks.' 'Why? They're both in order. Are you thinking of buying them? How did you get hold of them?' 'Very simple – I got them from you. My friend filled them in.' 'Go on! With all the stamps?' 'Of course.' 'Well, I'll be damned! Tell your friend from me that he's a great artist. You'll get through any checkpoint anywhere in the Reich with these. There's no better ID than a service passbook. Of course, it won't get you out of the country. But then again, no Germans can get out of the country.' 'One more question – what do you think of the handwriting in Hans Brück's passbook? It's not like an army clerk's, is it? You need really good handwriting to do that job, surely.' 'Oh well, they're not so fussy about handwriting these days. They're quite happy if a soldier can write at all.' When Ludwig reported all this back to me, I was greatly relieved. I was no longer afraid to venture out into the streets, particularly now I had my bike.

Dr Meier was thrilled with my passbook. But he found my plan of escaping to Switzerland childish. 'Schönhaus, everybody who tries it gets caught, even before they're anywhere near the border. Why do you want to take the risk? With papers like these and a place like the Waldstrasse to stay, you've got nothing to fear. What more do you want? Making for Switzerland just like that – it's bound to go wrong. If you really must try for Switzerland, there are better ways of doing it. I'll probably opt to do so myself eventually.'

'What ways are there, then?' 'I know a conductor on the Reich railway. He works on the route from Berlin to Basel. For a thousand marks he'll mark the back of my ticket, and shortly before the frontier I'll go with him to the luggage van. The luggage van travels on from the last German station to a Swiss one.' 'Have you checked up on this conductor's promise, Dr Meier?' 'Why? He seems pretty reliable to me. You're being very cautious about my plan all of a sudden, Schönhaus, but you don't mind risking a bike ride to Switzerland.' 'That's right, Dr Meier – because going to Switzerland the way I plan, my fate is in my own hands, aside from God's. In the case of the railway conductor you'd be trusting someone you hardly know. Hold on, we could check up on him, if you like – we could do it here and now on your telephone. Do you mind?'

I went to the phone. 'Hello, can I have German Railways, please? Fräulein, I'd like some information. I am a diplomat and I'm due to travel from Berlin to Switzerland. I have a question: I am taking a lot of suitcases with me. Does the luggage van continue with the train into Switzerland? Yes, find out for me please! I see – luggage vans don't leave German territory. Then my luggage will have to be taken across by taxi to the Swiss station. Thank you very much. Heil Hitler!'

Dr Meier was stunned. 'So, the railway official really is a con man, Schönhaus. We would have been arrested. You've saved our lives.' 'Well, look at it this way: I have you to thank for putting me in touch with Ludwig, and indirectly for getting me my new passbook. So we're quits.'

On the way back to the Waldstrasse, I stopped off at Tatjana's. She was very sad to hear I was leaving. But I could not have stayed at her place, anyway. Of late, she had become very friendly with the concierge's wife, who now spent a lot of time sitting around in Tatjana's flat. But there was one thing she wanted to do for me. 'Listen – you've lost your ID once already.' She was already at work on her sewing machine, and in no time at all had run up a purse made of red flowery material to hang round my neck. 'So that you don't lose your pass again!' 'Good idea,' I said. If there was a check, it would be better to grope awkwardly for the passbook in my purse, rather than whip it out smartly from a trouser pocket. With the purse I looked like an over-protected mummy's boy, rather than a notorious passport forger trying to escape over the border. 'Many thanks, Tatjana.' We said our goodbyes; I knew she didn't really believe I would risk it.

It was already dark. I pedalled through the Nettelbeckplatz, a district that had taken quite a hammering in the last air raid. Only façades were left standing, like theatre scenery; black façades with many holes where windows had been. It was doubly quiet because nobody was living there any more. Suddenly I heard a voice, ringing out as though from a stage. From within the empty masonry the echo rang out twice as loud: 'Ja, ja, ja, ja, ja. That's what they all voted for.'[47] And then, singing: 'Ja, ja, ja, ja, ja. But now? Where are they now? Jawohl, jawohl, jawohl. What has become of them? Jawohl, jawohl, jawohl.' The voice reverberated in the darkness. There was not a soul in sight. But the sing-song speech sounded wonderfully theatrical.

I cycled over to Frau Zukale's and picked up three white shirts I had left there. Now there was nothing holding me back. Ludwig stood at the door looking at the sky. 'It's a bomber's moon, Schönhaus. They could come back tonight.'

The beginning of the end in Berlin –
6 September 1943

I lay on the couch in the shop. My steel stallion stood nearby, saddled up and raring to go. The knapsack was strapped to it. A thread hanging from the hollow handlebar pulled out a cork, bringing with it four sheets of paper headed AEG. Every sheet was a leave certificate in the name of Hans Brück, technical draughtsman. Each leave certificate was valid for a week. I could produce the appropriate one for each week.

I was lying there trying to work out what would happen if I was stopped by a policeman: 'Hey, you there, young man – why aren't you in the military?' Answer: 'I've been conscripted as a technical draughtsman. I've got a week's leave.' Question: 'Where do you work?' Answer: 'AEG, armaments factory. I'm in a reserved occupation. Here's my leave certificate.' Question: 'Where are you heading?' Answer: 'Just touring.' Question: 'Why on a bicycle and not by rail?' Answer: 'A self-respecting German lad doesn't use trains. Wheels must roll for victory.'

While I was still thinking up the questions I might have to face, Ludwig shook me. 'Get up, Schönhaus – air-raid warning!' 'Yes, I know, Ludwig, I heard it ages ago.' We both stood at the open door looking out on the Waldstrasse. There was no one to be seen. Only a stray dog. I looked up. I couldn't remember who wrote it, but a sentence came to mind: 'The starry skies above me, and the moral law within . . .' There was an armada of bombers thundering over our heads. You couldn't see them, but they were coming closer all the time.

'Schönhaus, it's going to get rough tonight. I'm going to pull

down the iron shutter on the shop window. Move your bike a bit further away from the window. Can you see the green lights dropping? Right overhead? Those are what the British use to mark their target zone.' The drone got louder. The air was vibrating, the window panes rattling. Yet still there was nothing to be seen. 'Perhaps they're going to pass over, after all?' 'No, no, can't you hear that faint whistling?' It was louder now, a crescendo. 'Let's get to the back of the shop!'

There was a sound like a hurricane and then an ear-splitting explosion. The window was shattered, and the iron shutter bent outwards. Then more whistling, closer and closer. That was the next bomb. After the crash, white fog drifted from the street into the shop. My bike and my desk had both been thrown across the room. But there was no damage. My forger's kit (I had omitted the eyelet-punch, of course) was safe in the knapsack. The third bomb was already whistling down. A shower of sparks hissed out in the street. 'Those are incendiaries, Ludwig! First of all they send off fireworks, and then, once they've died down, you have to be careful. That's when the blazing liquid phosphorus explodes. It sticks and goes on burning, and at first you can only put it out with sand. You can't put water on it until afterwards, otherwise it explodes.' 'My God, Schönhaus, how do you know all that?' 'I had to do an air-raid warden course when I was working for Anton Erdmann.'

'Watch out, there's another one coming! Come on, Schönhaus – before the building collapses. Let's get under the arch of that sealed-up doorway to the shopkeeper's house. If the whole place comes down, maybe the door arch will hold out. Or better still, let's break down the door. Otherwise we may never get out of here.' 'What about the people living in there? Officially we aren't even here.' 'It doesn't matter. Come on, let's break the door down with this axe.'

We clambered through the splintered door. Five women were sitting on chairs leaning against the wall. They were astonished to see us. 'Thank God there are still men in the building.' None of them asked any questions. 'It's probably best if we all go to the air-raid cellar,' I said. We had never seen anything like it. It was the first big air raid on Berlin.

I couldn't stand it in the cellar any longer. Waiting, waiting, waiting. What for? Ludwig had already gone back up. I followed him. In the yard, near the top of the cellar stairs, lay a red bomb. A dud. The bomb lay there peacefully, as red as a fire extinguisher, a pointed cone at the front, and four fins at the back. It was no more than a metre long. I stepped over it gingerly.

We went out through the arch of the courtyard on to the street. Cows had broken loose from their shed and were

running wild in the road. There were places right in the middle of Berlin where they still kept cows for fresh milk. The cows were fed on potato peelings; old men used to come into the courtyards ringing a bell and shouting: 'Firewood for potato peel.' The women came down with bags full of potato peelings in exchange for kindling to light their briquette-burning stoves. But now the cows would not be getting any more potato peelings, only terror. They were new to the inferno. They raced through the streets; their mooing sounding like Viking war horns.

We looked at our shop from the outside. The iron shutter was bent outwards in a big curve, but apart from that, the building had not suffered too much damage. The bombs had

174

landed a few metres away. But through a broken window on the first floor we could see sparks flying. We raced upstairs two steps at a time. There were two buckets on the landing, one of water and one of sand. First we poured sand on to the incendiary hissing away in the room, and then water, just as I had been trained to do.

It seemed no time before the air-raid warden came up the stairs, complete with steel helmet, gasmask attached to his belt. 'You did well there, lads. Do you want to come up to the roof with me?' The long-drawn-out sound of the all-clear siren was wailing by this time. 'Yes, we'll come up with you.' Nobody asked who we were or what we were doing there. We surveyed a sea of flames. It was an odd feeling – should I be scared, or should I enjoy myself, like Nero as Rome burned? It's a judgement on them, I thought. But could one crime cancel out another, like balancing account books? Or was it ultimately simply a matter of two crimes? War is always cruel. Yet how could the worst murderer of all time be stopped except by war?

I went out into the road. Cows were still racing around in the darkness. A firestorm was sending paper, leaves and burnt scraps whirling through the air. Five-storey buildings were ablaze on all four street corners. Strangely, fire spread from the cellar upwards, eating its way from floor to floor until it reached the roof.

The Waldstrasse was wide, with a carriageway on either side divided by a promenade planted with maples which ran down the middle. The promenade was now chock full of people and household goods. There were lamps, armchairs, suitcases, and a birdcage with two budgerigars perched on top of them all. And then there were mattresses. Women, children and old men stood around. Hardly any able-bodied men to lend a hand. But there was one; he was yelling at his wife: 'Let the stuff burn – you're not going into that building again.

You're staying here. You'll have a beam falling on your head. No, stay here, I tell you! D'you hear me?' An elderly man was wandering up and down aimlessly. I remarked to him in passing: 'Terrible, isn't it?' He stopped, said not a word, turned away, and left.

The sky was slowly lightening. The sun began to shine. I picked up my bike and checked whether there was still air in the tyres. Everything was OK. The knapsack was still firmly fastened to the luggage carrier. Ludwig's face was completely soot-blackened. Mine too, probably. We laughed. I had a wash in the courtyard. Then we looked at each other. 'I suppose I should be making a start. What do you think?' 'Yes, I would go while the bike is still usable, Schönhaus. And here, I nearly forgot.' He reached into his trouser pocket and pulled out a hundred-franc note. 'This is something for your new start in Switzerland.' He was gone before I could thank him.

My bike had to be carried more than pushed. The road was full of fire hoses and shards of glass. At the corner they were still putting out fires. However, ten streets away I was able to mount. It seemed as though no raid had taken place there at all. My bike rolled along. The slipstream cooled my face.

Everyone living underground in Berlin and never venturing out of doors believed that the city was hemmed in, and that anybody trying to get out to the countryside would run into a police checkpoint. But in reality I cycled along a car-free highway. Apart from squirrels darting across the road, and the noisy starlings flocking together, there was no other sign of life. No one bothered about me. From the bridge in Pichelsberg I took a last look down at my boat in Paul Böhm's marina. It lay bare of rigging, dreaming alongside its mooring buoy. I followed the signposts to Potsdam.

Potsdam, town of the kings of Prussia, glittered in the

sunshine. Frederick the Great's barouche once rolled over the cobbles there. The houses of his royal officials stood spick and span next to the Garrison Church, the same church whose bells played the venerable tune of 'Üb immer Treu und Redlichkeit' (Be loyal and be upright, Unto your grave so cold, So that with your earthly might, To God's own path you hold). It was to this tune that the Bohemian corporal (Hitler) publicly duped Reich President Paul von Hindenburg by masquerading as the successor of Frederick the Great.[48] Loyalty and uprightness were no more, but for countless numbers of people there remained the grave so cold.

In Beelitz the sight of an inn reminded me that I had not eaten all day. I hadn't slept the previous night, either. So at that moment I had no objection to pea soup with bacon cubes and croutons.

The road I was taking led to Wittenberg, the town of Luther, the first stopover on my journey to Switzerland. Would I make it? I wasn't in too much of a hurry. For the time being, I could enjoy my pea soup.

That evening, after almost a hundred kilometres, I walked into the hotel Zur Traube and registered quite normally as Hans Brück. I was given a room with a glorious bed, and slept the dreamless sleep of the just. What had I done to deserve this?

Where am I actually heading?

I had been used to moving around in the world in illicit ways since I was fourteen. In 1936, to the horror of my parents, I went on an excursion with the Hashomer Hatzair, a left-leaning, Jewish youth organization. Going on a trip didn't mean going by train. No, we preferred hitch-hiking. We wore boots, white shirts, and white socks, and we carried Hitler Youth knapsacks.

Everything about us was prohibited: our gear, the organization, and hitch-hiking – especially on the autobahn, out of bounds even for German youngsters. But that didn't stop us from thumbing a lift from a black Mercedes. We were taken aback to see a high-ranking SA leader sitting there with his driver. 'All right, lads, where do you want to go?' 'To Cologne.' 'And are you in the Hitler Youth?' 'Yessir.' 'Right, jump in then.' And so the black Mercedes drove us to Cologne. We didn't mention this at home, of course. If we had, that would have been our last trip. But that exercise in illegality served me well now.

There was a policeman on the other side of the highway, riding a bicycle like me. His uniform was green; he was a *Gendarm*, a rural policeman. I became aware of him suddenly as he looked across at me and waved. Aha, I thought, here we go: my first police check. But he merely called out: 'Can't you see I'm using a clearly marked cycle path, and you're not?' 'But I thought you always had to keep to the right.' 'Not when there's a marked cycle path on the left! Remember that.' He turned off at the next crossroads.

Where was I actually going? Of course I wasn't just touring at random. No: Claus Schiff was a nice chap, and he had reconnoitred my entry route into Switzerland by making a special trip to Feldkirch. At the station in Feldkirch they loaded a goods train every day with coal bound for Switzerland. From a wooded embankment next to the track it was easy to see when the last carriage was being coupled up. 'That's the moment to go down,' he had said. 'Stand next to the line, not too near the station. As the train passes, you just jump on, preferably on to a wagon with a brakesman's cabin. Then you travel on to Switzerland with it. The train is not checked at the border.'

So I did know where I was going – to Feldkirch. I'd had practice at jumping off, and somehow I would manage to jump on. But right now what I had to do was bend my back and pedal, otherwise my head would hit one of the apples that hung from the trees, paradise-fashion. No one was picking them. The scarecrows in the fields did duty for the men who should have been doing the picking. The men had no time; they were too busy killing or being killed. And I was doing duty for the dead on my journey towards freedom – or maybe towards the next world. Only time would tell.

Meanwhile, though, I propped my bike against an apple tree, selected the crispest apple, lay down in the grass and recited: 'Mine host he is most generous, I'm sure you will allow, A golden apple is his sign, hung out upon a bough.' The juice ran down my chin, and I let the small slivers melt between my teeth. 'I asked him what there was to pay; he merely shook his crown. Long life to him say I, and may he never be cut down.'

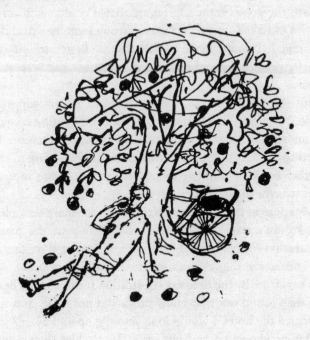

All right, I couldn't pay. But I could share. In a stationery shop in Bad Däuben I bought a box that held four apples. Then I went to the post office and sent them to Ludwig's wife, who was still living legally in Berlin. I enclosed a card bearing Friedrich Schiller's words: 'For a moment lived in paradise, death is not too high a price.'

I had a great deal to thank Ludwig for: first of all, the workshop in the Waldstrasse; then the army passbook; and finally the contact with Claus Schiff. The hundred-franc note was the gilt on the gingerbread. He even wanted me to take his pistol, but I declined. Shoot an innocent frontier guard just so that I could escape? I could imagine him lying in front of me, and hear his death rattle. I would find pictures of his wife and children in his wallet. And I would be his murderer. No, I could get across the frontier without that. I could leap aboard the goods train. Or, failing that, I could swim across an arm of Lake Constance. I was a strong swimmer. And if all else failed, I could make a dash for it. Better to get shot myself, because everything else in store for me was much worse.

But meanwhile I was looking forward to my supper in Halle. Yes, I even had Ludwig to thank for the ration coupons for my trip. If I had used them all up by mid-September but failed to get across the border by then, he was going to send another book of coupons to Lindau for me, poste restante. That was the arrangement.

My room in the hotel Zum Krug was once more very pleasant. I didn't wait for the waitress to bring me the pad of registration forms; I asked for it myself. I wanted to give her the impression that everything about me was in order. And that was true. By the time my registration form reached Berlin and they found out that Hans Brück did not exist, and then informed the hotel, I would long since be up and away.

Having showered and put on a clean white shirt, I went

down to the restaurant. In contrast to the hotel Zur Traube in Wittenberg, where I had been the only one eating, here the dining room was almost full. They were all soldiers. A place was found for me at a table where three troopers were already sitting. 'Have a seat, comrade,' said one of them, pushing a chair towards me. 'We're on a training exercise here. But at least we're getting a decent meal this evening. A change from that muck they serve from the field kitchen. Otherwise, it's quite a cushy number. Apart from poor old Horst, who has to lug his flame thrower around with him like a rucksack.' 'Yeah, yeah,' said Horst, 'but when I give 'em a blast, they're all finished. Dead ducks. Makes it worth while.' 'And what about you, comrade, not in the forces?' 'No, I've been con-scripted and deferred. I'm a technical draughtsman with AEG.' 'But sooner or later they'll pull you in.' 'I don't think so. I've got lung trouble, you see.' 'That's good. I could do with something like that. Well, eat up, comrades, food's get-ting cold.'

Next morning at breakfast I read in the paper that yet another Jew had been caught trying to reach Switzerland. He was sleeping in the cornfields by day, and making his way south at night. Schoolchildren alerted the police.

With my knapsack securely strapped on, I too travelled southwards. Although it was 10 September, the sun burned as hot as in midsummer. I came to a bridge, marked SAALE. So that's the river we used to sing about in school: 'By the Saale's gleaming shores, Stand castles proud and bold. Their rafters soon will fall, And the winds blow through the hall, And clouds pass over grey and cold.' It occurred to me I could take a dip here.

I stopped. Good idea. Why shouldn't I? Except that I didn't have any swimming trunks. I looked around; not a soul in sight, apart from two farm girls who were binding sheaves on the opposite bank. I undressed. The girls walked towards each other and waved. I waved back. The air was warm, but the water was cold. If I did swim across Lake Constance at night, I would take a fully inflated inner tube with me from my bike, so I could swim quietly, with economical movements. My swim now was a kind of training session. When I got out of the water neither of the girls looked at me. They had seen a naked young man before.

When I was about ten years old, a street vendor used to stand outside our school with a box full of slips of paper in front of him, and a budgerigar perched on the side of it. On the box was written: 'Five pfennigs for the budgie to pick your lucky number.' I gave him a five-pfennig piece, and received a slip of paper with the numbers three, five, seven and nine.

I had just spotted Bamberg in the distance, and was suddenly feeling scared, which was why my lucky numbers came to mind. I was badly in need of some luck. What was the point of buying the lucky numbers, after all, if they weren't going to come in useful now? The numbers became a magic game. There were numbers on every telegraph pole, and every number acquired personal significance. For example, here was the number 18-732. The eighteen was made up of twice nine. Seven was one of my lucky numbers anyway. The last two numbers not only included a three, but added up to another lucky number, five. I drew my conclusion: Cioma would get to Switzerland.

Then there was the registration number of a truck that was overtaking me: 1A63782. 63=9x7, which was very good. The seven was fine anyway. And eight and two make ten, which is to say twice five; lucky again. End result: nothing but good luck! I was going to succeed. The more numbers I came across – house numbers, telephone numbers, price tickets, and so forth – the more convinced I was that I would survive. I really believed that I would save and nurse the spark of life my parents had left behind in me, and fan it to a flame in a world where 'Good morning' actually meant you wished somebody a good morning. If any figures cropped up that I couldn't somehow break down into my lucky numbers, I simply ignored them.

In Bamberg I stopped at the hotel Zum Bamberger Reiter. The guests sat at their tables listening with rapt attention, staring transfixed at the loudspeaker. A special news bulletin had been announced – without victory fanfares this time. The Führer spoke. He had sent in SS Obersturmbannführer (Lieutenant-Colonel) Otto Skorzeny[49] to rescue his friend, Benito Mussolini,[50] in a lightning commando raid. The Duce was on his way to Führer headquarters. The treatment of the Italian traitors would be what we expected from National Socialists – cold, ruthless and without mercy. The Führer's friends knew they could count on him. And Heil Hitler. The hotel guests listened silently.

The next day I travelled on with a following wind towards Stuttgart. I planned to visit Pastor Kurt Müller there; I had always been impressed by this vigorous man on his visits to Berlin. It was good that such Germans existed. 'That's why you can enjoy your trip through this beautiful country, Cioma, in spite of everything. And why you can even feel at home here.' Rosa Luxemburg said once: 'I feel at home wherever there are clouds, birds and human tears.' There were human tears in Germany, too.

In Stuttgart I went to a baker's shop before visiting Pastor Müller, and bought two pieces of apple cake on my ration coupons. Holding the cake, I rang at the door. 'My goodness, Schönhaus! Fancy seeing you here!' He gave me a powerful hug. He looked at me as though I had returned from the dead. Tears ran down his face. 'Schönhaus, I was convinced you'd all been arrested. When I ring Helene Jacobs and Dr Kaufmann, all I hear is the voice of a police agent. They're very keen to know who I am. When I ask them in return "and who are you?" they lose interest in any further conversation. But come in, come in.' I asked him how he was. 'The fact that you've survived is a chink of light. But currently I'm suffering from toothache and bile-duct colic.' At his words the heavens opened in a cloud-burst, accompanied by lightning and thunder. The Pastor shook his fist at the sky: 'Don't *Thou* start, as well!' We both laughed.

The walls of the Pastor's living room were painted white – what could be seen of them, because they were almost hidden behind a wealth of books. A baroque timepiece with two weights and a long pendulum hung where a bit of white wall peeped out. Its regular ticking conveyed peace. The world was torn apart by war, yet here you would never know it.

While he was a pastor in peasant guise, his wife was an elfin sprite. She brought us cups of malt coffee, and joined us. 'You'll spend the night here, of course.' They both wanted to know how many times I had been checked. 'Never,' I said, 'not once. I was surprised myself. And I was looking forward to putting my service passbook to the test.' 'Passbook? Let me see. Good heavens, I must show this to my friend Vorster! Let's go over and see him in Degerloch later. I want to introduce you to him. You know, lots of people come here to go underground, or to try to get to Switzerland. Most of them haven't got a chance, I'm afraid. Unfortunately, they're not always the most likeable people. It's no trouble at all to help a likeable person. Helping unlikeable people – that's hard work.'

We went by tram to Degerloch. I always imagined pastors dressed in black, with a dog collar. Pastor Müller was something of an exception, but it was an even bigger surprise to see a *Wehrmacht* NCO advancing towards me, clicking his heels and announcing himself as 'Pastor Vorster'. He was an army chaplain. He was sitting in the garden with his wife. Pastor Müller introduced me. 'This is Hans Brück. He stayed at Helene Jacobs's place and forged all those passes I kept taking to Berlin from the two of us. The group was arrested, but he managed to escape, and he's cycled here from Berlin.'

He turned to me: 'Show him your passbook.' I produced it. 'Well, so what? It's just a passbook like any other. What's so special about it?' 'Goodness, Vorster, it came to him blank, and he filled it in himself, complete with all the stamps.' 'My word – show me again. And you're a Jew? Living illegally? And what now?' 'Now I want to go to Switzerland.'

'Can you believe it – his papers weren't checked once, all the way from Berlin to Stuttgart. Well, he doesn't exactly look like a Jew on the run, does he?' 'This is something to cheer about at last, Kurt,' said Pastor Vorster. And to me he said: 'I'm impressed. Tell me exactly how it all came about.' He asked his wife to get supper for us. 'One thing is definite – you're going to spend the night here. My study is at your disposal. You're staying too, Kurt. This visit has got to be celebrated.'

We sat on white garden chairs, and there was bread, ham and eggs on the table. With it we drank red wine, *Spätburgunder*. As darkness fell, we talked by candlelight. 'I'm crossing my fingers for you, Schönhaus, and hoping you make it. But we'll miss you.' Who could have foreseen this pleasant gathering?

I was tired, and ready to turn in. The pastor's wife had made up a bed for me in the study. Only after she said good night did it occur to me that I'd forgotten to ask where the lavatory was. I thought about the window as an emergency measure. But they would have heard the tinkling sound. In the end I found a large flower vase. I groped my way down to the kitchen with it and poured the contents down the sink.

Marvellously rested, I woke up next morning to find the

table laid for breakfast, as though by magic. A jovial Pastor Vorster greeted me in the German manner with a handshake, as if he had just returned from a long journey. 'My dear Schönhaus,' he began, 'why don't you just stay here with us? With that passbook nothing can happen to you. But trying to cross the frontier into Switzerland is one of the worst crimes, even for us Aryans. You could stay with us until the war is over, whereas if they pick you up at the border, things will be bad for you.'

'It's a tempting offer, Herr Vorster. But you're forgetting that I'm a wanted man – twice over; as Günther Rogoff the pass-forger, and as Peter Petrov, the alleged Russian spy. And they have a recent passport photo. I respect your willingness to take the risk of hiding me. But I don't want to expose you to that danger. The war could go on for a long time yet. France is still occupied, and the *Wehrmacht* is still deep into Russia. And the Nazis never run short of personnel for hunting people down, however tough the fighting becomes. No, I'll spend my last night in Stuttgart in a hotel, so that I don't risk betraying anyone who has sheltered me. I'm hoping to get across the frontier, but you have to reckon with things going wrong. That's why it's good to cover yourself beforehand. All the same, many thanks for the offer.'

A short time later Pastor Müller came and collected me again, and we went back to his house by tram. 'You were wondering whether I'd manage to jump aboard the moving goods train in Feldkirch? Just watch this. I've been in training.' I jumped off the moving tram, raced alongside it for a few paces, and leapt back on again. Kurt Müller shook his head. 'Now I believe you.'

I picked up my bike at his place. To cover my tracks, I planned to spend the night in a hotel: the Anker looked respectable, exactly the place for me. I had just put my knapsack down on the bed and was about to go downstairs to register in the proper fashion, when there was a knock at the door. 'Herr Brück?' When I opened up, my heart nearly stopped. Facing me was a tall man in a grey leather coat and trilby – a typical Gestapo figure. How could this have happened? I hadn't even registered at the hotel yet. They might know that a guest had arrived, but they couldn't know my name.

The man at the door introduced himself: 'My name is Pastor Baumgartner. I've come especially from Berlin to see you. Pfarrer Müller told me where to find you. I need your help urgently. It's about a pass that has to be altered. Could you do that before you leave?' My mouth was still dry. 'Herr Pastor, let me ask you a question: could you see how shocked I was?' 'No, what do you mean? I didn't notice anything.' 'Well, that's comforting. I now know that I can afford to be as shocked as I like. It doesn't show.'

We went downstairs to the desk, and I registered. Then we went back to Kurt Müller's place.

My first checkpoint

When I parted from Pastor Müller he looked me deep in the eye, pressed my hand firmly, and said with a choking voice: 'God keep you.' It was like a leave-taking for ever. A shiver ran down my spine. All very different from my goodbyes to Pastor Vorster. He had shaken my hand and said: 'And when you get to Basel, give my regards to Karl Barth. He believes in me, and that gives me courage.'

My faithful bike was coasting along almost by itself. It was downhill now to Lake Constance. Just outside Lindau there was a soldier in the middle of the road. His helmet had slipped slightly to the back of his head. I could see his reddish-blond hair. His rifle swung loosely from his shoulder. He stopped me as I approached. 'Halt, where are you going?' 'Feldkirch,' I said simply. 'Your ID!' I pulled out Tatjana's purse from around my neck and showed him my passbook. The soldier, a farm lad, leafed through it and compared the photograph with me. Finally he returned the passbook with the words: 'Carry on, Herr Schmidt.' I stifled a laugh. The youngster had not even worked out my name: Schmidt was the signature of the local military commander. My name in the pass was Hans Brück. But I forbore to correct him as he waved me on with an 'all in order'.

The hotel Zum Löwen (The Lion) in Feldkirch lived up to its name. It was a massive building, built to last for ever. My room looked like a large cell in a well-appointed convent. The dining room was huge. So was my appetite. Next morning I went to the station. Everything was exactly as Claus Schiff had described it: a vast marshalling yard where trains were made up. One was being loaded with coal obviously intended for Switzerland. When it moved, I would leap aboard it and hide in the brakesman's cabin. The train would then travel unchecked over the frontier. That was the procedure explored for me by Claus Schiff. But it wasn't going to be quick: it could take until the afternoon to couple up all those wagons.

On the wooded embankment overlooking the station, I sat down on some grass behind a tree. From there I could watch the game of shunting the goods wagons to and fro. To pass the time I cut a thick branch that I could whittle into a decorated walking stick. By the time I'd finished it looked like a totem pole out of a Karl May story. Noon came. The train with coal for Switzerland was only very slowly increasing in length. It would be hours before it was ready to depart. I was sure I would have time to eat in the hotel Zum Löwen.

A white tablecloth. A young secretary from the hotel on her day off sat opposite me. She was very attractive, and flashing her blue eyes at me in such a way that I thought: 'You've got a hotel room, and perhaps this is the last chance you will ever have in your life to feel the warmth of a young woman.' When I touched her hand, she did not take it away.

But then, like a sign from God, the sirens began to wail. What? An air-raid warning here in Feldkirch? That was impossible. But an air-raid warning it was. We went outside on to the big terrace. High up in the sky we saw the vapour trails of the American Flying Fortresses. And suddenly I heard the familiar whistling sound of bombs getting nearer. Everyone raced for the stairs down to the air-raid shelter. I took the secretary's hand. But suddenly she gave a cry: 'My handbag! I've left it hanging on the chair!' Heroically, I ran back to the dining room, picked up her bag, and was rewarded with a kiss. I could hear explosions coming from somewhere in the town.

The sirens sounded the all-clear. In two senses. 'Cioma,' I said to myself, 'don't get sidetracked. You want to make it to Switzerland. You want to jump aboard the goods train. Don't be stupid; don't fritter away your time. Do what you intended. The air-raid warning was a clear signal. Go back to the railway embankment. The fir trees will hide you from the prying eyes of policemen guarding the area.'

By the evening I could see the train slowly being completed. They were attaching the last wagons. It would surely leave soon. I went down unhurriedly, moved towards the line, and waited for the train. It came hissing towards me. So far I had only known trains pulled by steam engines, which took a long time to accelerate, so that you could run alongside them on a platform for quite some distance. But this was an electric locomotive, and it built up speed rapidly. The wagons rushed past me at a pace that ruled out leaping on board. I stood there appalled and disappointed. But I told myself: 'You can try again tomorrow, but nearer to the station, where the train hasn't yet picked up so much speed.'

So, another night in the Lion's den. No sign of the secretary. Next morning was bright and cheerful, with plenty of sunshine, blue skies, and an Austrian breakfast. I strolled down to the embankment again. Suddenly there was a man barring my path. '*Parla italiano?*' 'No,' I said, shaking my head. 'Where you go?' 'Why?' 'I see you yesterday. Whole day on embankment. And German soldiers see you too. They look for you in evening. I want only warn you.' '*Grazie mille, amico.*' '*Prego, prego.*'

I went quickly back to the hotel, paid the bill, and disappeared. I retraced my route around Lake Constance. I had hopped off the gravedigger's spade once more, as the Berliners say. How many more lives did I have left? 'Who is keeping a constant eye on you? Who is helping you to keep up your courage? Who is helping you to disarm others by your friendliness? Who is telling you in this horrible time to create a memorial for the other Germans, the ones prepared to give their lives to save Jews?'

I had to forget the Feldkirch goods train route. I had two remaining plans: either to swim across Lake Constance at night, at the point where it was only a kilometre wide; or I could try crossing the frontier in the Schiener Berg area, at the western end of the lake. I knew the place from studying the General Staff map with Sister Thesi.

My bike rolled along in the warm summer wind, on the road running around Lake Constance. The lake had a silvery glitter, just as described in Horst Wolfram Geissler's book *Lieber Augustin*. I was whistling tunes from Brecht's *Threepenny Opera*: 'Yes, make a hopeless plan, to show how bright you are. And then think up another one, that gets you just as far.' I had to think up another plan.

The road, flooded with sunlight, was completely empty. I was alone on my bike and could talk to myself out loud. I tried to imagine who would check my papers next, and what sort of person he would be. Let's assume a smart young policeman. A stickler for detail. What would he ask me? 'Your ID, please.' Good, that was no problem. But then: 'Where are you travelling to?' 'Öhningen.' 'And where have you come from?' 'From Berlin.' 'By bicycle? Then it would take you a week to get here.' 'I took the train to Lindau, and put my bike in the guard's van.' 'Yes, exactly. If you've only got a fortnight's leave from AEG, you would have had to start back straight away otherwise. But where are you heading for? Öhningen, of all places. That's right on the Swiss border.' 'Yes, I've been invited to go there.' 'Who by?' – Yes, who by? It was a good question! But I could devise an answer over lunch. At the next inn I would ask for the phone book.

I turned in at the hotel Zum Zeppelin and found a window seat with a view of the lake. I ordered lake trout and a telephone book. Excellent – Öhningen was in it. There was a name there I really liked: Ferdinand Schmidt, landowner, Stuttgart Court. That was where I was headed! While I spooned my cauliflower soup, I conjured up a vision of Ferdinand. Ferdinand Lassalle, the first Social Democrat in Germany. What's more, he was a Jew. So 'Ferdinand' was good. Then the policeman would go on to ask me: 'Who is this Herr Schmidt, then? How do you know him? And why are you going there?' 'My boss at AEG, Herr Faber, gave me this recommendation for my journey. "Herr Brück," he said, "take the train to Lindau, with the bike in the guard's van. And then go and visit my friend Schmidt in Öhningen. Give him my best regards. I'm sure you'll be able to spend a few days of your holiday on his farm."' In conjunction with my passbook and the leave confirmation from AEG, that should be enough to satisfy the most suspicious of policemen.

But nobody checked me. It was getting dark, so I stopped off at the hotel Zum Adler. In bed I continued to think about what sort of person Ferdinand Schmidt was. Perhaps he was an old Social Democrat. Yes, perhaps he was even a supporter of the Confessing Church, who knew Karl Barth. That would be great. As I gave my fantasy free rein, a plan took shape in my mind: I really would visit Herr Schmidt. I kept the film running through my head: I saw myself ringing at the door of his country house. Ferdinand Schmidt opens it. 'Hello, Herr Schmidt. My name is Hans Brück. I've come from Berlin. My boss at AEG, Herr Faber, gave me your address. He sends his regards. I'm wondering if I could spend a few days of my holiday . . .' 'Young man, I don't know any Herr Faber at AEG, but all the same I think I know what you want. First of all, come in and have a bowl of soup with us. And then after dark I'll show you the way over the border. You're not the first to turn up here.'

My wish-fulfilment dream sent me off to sleep. There was a knock on the door at four in the morning. 'Open up. Police!' It was a *Gendarm*. His torch was shining into my face, blinding me. 'Your passbook, chum!' My red purse lay underneath my clothes on the chair. The constable leafed through the passbook, page by page. Then he gave it back to me. 'All in order. Heil Hitler.' I slept until ten.

Man proposes, God disposes

'God decides the major part of what happens to you, Cioma. But you are responsible for the minor part. And you have to carry out this minor part with your brains, with your talents, and with your belief in help from above.' Then I heard the pounding of the wheels of the train to Majdanek.

> What's going to happen . . . don't think about it . . . don't
> think about it . . .
> What's going to happen . . . don't think about it . . . don't
> think about it . . .
> What's going to happen . . . don't think about it . . . don't
> think about it . . . We'll be helping you.

I was almost freewheeling downhill towards Öhningen. I passed a nursery where a woman was cutting flowers. When a well-bred young German is invited anywhere, he takes flowers with him. 'You can buy a bouquet here,' I said to myself. 'It will be a good accessory. And it suggests the exact opposite of a Jew trying to escape into Switzerland.' My shorts, the military haircut, and the Hitler Youth knapsack completed the look. The nursery gardener assembled the bouquet lovingly, as though she knew what it was for. And with the bouquet fixed between the handlebars and the headlamp, my bike ran along even more sweetly.

An SS man stood at the side of the road, rifle on shoulder, chatting to a girl. Both threw friendly glances after me. I came to the place-name sign for Öhningen, and asked an old man where Stuttgart Court was. 'First left, and then straight on. Only about ten minutes by bike.' 'Thanks.' I pushed on. In a meadow in the distance, tiny, fluttering in the wind, there was a Swiss flag. My heart began to race: it was the first time in my life I had seen one flying freely in the open air.

'Cioma,' I said to myself, 'you could just cycle over the grass now and be in Switzerland. No, Cioma! It's not that easy. There are bell wires at the frontier, and border guards with dogs. If you tried to dash across here you wouldn't get far. Try acting out your scenario with Schmidt the landowner first. Perhaps he really is the kindly Social Democrat of your dreams. Maybe he will welcome the chance to oppose the cruelty of the regime by helping a Jew to escape. Who knows?'

I dismounted outside the country house, and rang. Nobody answered. I rang again. Still no answer. So I went across the courtyard, past a small building, and called out: 'Hello, any-body there?' A door opened, and a German soldier came out. His tunic was unbuttoned, his head bare. 'Hey, what are you doing here – have you got any ID?' 'Yes, I have!' I opened my shirt, took out the red purse, and showed him my passbook. 'Oh, we've got a service passbook, have we? That's all right, then. Where are you trying to get to?' 'I'm here to see the Schmidts, but nobody's answering the door.' 'Well, they are at home.' 'But I rang twice. Nobody came to the door.' 'Perhaps they're still asleep. Where have you come from, anyway?

From Berlin? I see. The Schmidts' son happens to be in Berlin at the moment. But come into our parlour. You know, we've got to write everything down. A load of red tape. Pure formality. But orders is orders.'

Inside there were three more soldiers. Four rifles stood in a rack by the wall. My soldier took out a form and began to copy from my passbook. Like a policeman, letter by letter. I chatted as casually as I could. 'Actually I'm a graphic artist. But in wartime I've been seconded from the military to work as a technical draughtsman with AEG.' Looking up from his writing and pointing to one of his comrades, he said: 'He's a graphic artist, too. He painted that picture on the wall.' I turned round to look at it. 'That's good! You've got talent.'

He had practically finished his writing. He stood up. 'Now you can go across to the Schmidts again. You just need to keep on ringing. It's a big house. They're certainly in.' At this moment another soldier came in, obviously returning from patrol, with helmet and rifle, and a furled rain cape slung across his chest. With a broad grin, my soldier said: 'There you go, Paul, another one for you. Take him in.' I joined in with his joking tone, laughingly slapping Paul on the shoulder and echoing what his comrade had said: 'Yes, Paul, you've got to take me in now.' They all laughed uproariously. 'All right, over you go to the Schmidts. They're definitely there.'

The soldiers disappeared into their guardroom. It didn't occur to any of them to follow me, to check up on my story about the visit. They left me alone to go across to the country house and ring.

This time the door actually did open. The man who opened it didn't look a bit like my fond image of him. He had a red beery face, a cross between Bismarck and Hindenburg, and wore a green hunting outfit, a hat with a chamois tuft, and puttees. He was obviously about to go hunting.

'Good morning. My name is Hans Brück and I've come from Berlin. Herr Faber, my boss at AEG, gave me your address.' I didn't even get to the part about spending a few days of my holiday etc, as he shouted back into the house: 'Hey, do you know any Faber in Berlin?' Frau Schmidt now came out and looked at me suspiciously. 'What are you doing up here? You'll be suspected of trying to get across the frontier!' 'Well, my papers have just been checked right here.' 'All right, but we don't know any Faber in Berlin. Perhaps you mean Dr Schmidt. He lives down in the village. They've got friends in Berlin. It must be them you want.' 'Oh, right. Well, I'm sorry to have disturbed you.'

Naturally, I held on to the bouquet, as I was supposedly proceeding to Dr Schmidt's in Öhningen. But two hundred metres further on there was a stream. According to my map it flowed across the frontier into Switzerland. I saw the Swiss flag again waving in the wind. 'Cioma,' I said to myself, 'sooner or later you've got to chance it.'

The forbidden frontier

I stopped at the stream. To make sure I couldn't continue my journey, I let the air out of my front tyre. Right. My mind was made up. I had burnt my bridges. I was thinking of removing the front wheel and taking it to the water. If anybody came along, I could say I had a puncture and was trying to locate the hole. But then I gave myself a talking to: 'Stop all these clever precautions, Cioma. If they haven't emerged from the bushes yet, that means there's nobody here. Make up your mind!'

I pulled on the thread in the handlebars, drew out my hundred-franc note, and pushed the bike into the bushes. Then, childlike, I prayed: '*Shemah Yisroel*: Hear O Israel, the Lord our God, the Lord is one.' I crawled on all fours along the stream. It was at most half a metre deep and a metre wide. At first I tried to stay in the sort of posture you adopt for press-ups, in order to keep as dry as possible. But suddenly I heard rifle shots. Instantly, staying dry was forgotten; it didn't matter any more. I ducked under, as far as I could in the shallow water, and scrambled on as fast as possible. I was hoping that this would throw the dogs off the scent.

At the time I didn't know that the 'shooting' was not aimed at me. It came from mechanical crop protectors that gave a loud bang at intervals to scare the birds off the grapes.

There was one thing I had firmly resolved: if they tried to

stop me, I would keep on going. I preferred to be shot, because I knew very well what to expect after my arrest and then in Poland. Better a terrible end than terror without end.

So I slithered along the stream. It seemed to go on for ever. According to my map it fed into a small pond, which was in Switzerland. But there was no sign of a pond. Then I reached a spot where the grass at the side of the stream had been mown. I guessed that this was the border; they wanted to keep a clear view here. I speeded up. My elbows were badly grazed, but I didn't notice. 'All right, just remember: if anybody appears or shouts "halt" – run for it.'

Suddenly I heard a noise. Right, start running! But I found myself stopping and putting my hands up. I was suddenly powerless to resist this reflex action. It is so hard to be a hero.

And as I stood there, a roe deer leapt out past me. That was what the noise was. But if I was standing there and nobody came, then it followed that there was nobody there. So I dashed on until the stream emptied into the pond – exactly as on the map.

One of my favourite books was *Robinson Crusoe*. I had never forgotten the passage where he is washed up on shore and sees that he is saved. So I followed his example, knelt down and kissed the earth.

I was in Switzerland.

I stepped on to Swiss soil in sopping-wet clothes, just as though that were a normal thing to do. People turned round to look at me. Women were out walking with men, not alone, as in Germany. Everything seemed peaceful and strange to me.

A bit further on I came to a sawmill, where I hid behind a pile of planks. I tried to dry my socks and shorts by wringing them out. A family was strolling past, and I heard a

It's so hard to be a hero!

young boy say in Swiss dialect: 'Daddy, there's a pair of shoes standing over there. I think there's someone there.' His father asked me what I was doing there. 'I'm a refugee from Germany.' 'I see. And I'm the cantonal policeman for Stein am Rhein. Get dressed. You can come home with me and have something to eat. We'll think about the next step tomorrow.'

As we walked along he asked me: 'Why did you escape?' 'Political,' I said. Pastor Müller had dinned into me that I mustn't say I was a Jew, or they would send me straight back. 'Political?' enquired the policeman. Suddenly, I'd had enough. Was I going to go on lying, even in Switzerland? The persecution had to stop somewhere. 'No, I want to tell you the truth. I'm a Jew.' 'All the same, I don't think they'll send you back,' said the cantonal policeman.

Next morning another policeman took me by train to Schaffhausen. My clothes were still wet, so I was wearing a waistcoat donated by the cantonal policeman. Since his size was at least a forty-six, it was flapping loosely around me. I must have looked rather pathetic, because another passenger whispered something to my guard. He nodded benevolently, and I was given a cigar and a light. In my enthusiasm I inhaled deeply a few times. Fortunately, it didn't make me sick.

There was another man standing in the prison waiting room. 'What have you done, then?' I asked him. My assumption was that in such times as ours, only decent people ended up in gaol. But he went red and didn't reply. 'Aha,' I thought, 'we're in Switzerland. Obviously, people in prison here actually deserve to be in prison.'

Then I was interrogated. Two police officers sat facing me. One of them bellowed at me: 'Your name isn't Schönhaus at all. You're a war criminal and you want to worm your way in here. Or you've been up to something else!' 'Dr Fliess or Professor Barth in Basel can vouch for me.' 'All a trick! We should just throw you out.'

Now it was my turn to flare up. 'If this goes on, I've had enough. Send me back if you want to. I didn't think Switzerland would be like this.' Now the other officer intervened. 'All right, that will do.' 'I've got a hundred francs here. Please telephone Dr Fliess for me.' 'Not necessary. You can save your money for something more important.' And to his colleague: 'And you, just calm down!'

Now I really was in Switzerland.

Thanks to Professor Barth I was given a grant to study. He had been fully informed about me by Pastor Kurt Müller in Stuttgart. After five years at the Basel School of Applied Art I finished my training as a graphic artist. I still practise my profession occasionally. I married, and have four sons. One is a graphic artist, another is a goldsmith, and the two youngest are musicians. I have four grandchildren and a wonderful wife. She was always a good mother, and now she is a resourceful grandmother. She has typed out my memories for this book several times over.

Helene Jacobs and I were friends for fifty years. She died on 27August 1993. She was honoured by Yad Vashem as one of the Righteous among the Nations.

Dorothee Fliess stayed on in Switzerland after she emigrated. She died in Basel in 2001.

Walter Heyman and Det Kassriel were deported.

Tatjana survived the war.

Stella Goldschlag's life has been depicted in books and films. Until her death she lived in seclusion in south-west Germany.

Ludwig Lichtwitz survived the war, and built up his father's printing works in Berlin again.

Dr Kaufmann was shot in Sachsenhausen.

Dr Meier was deported.

Gerda was deported.

As for my mother and father, Grandma, Aunt Sophie and Uncle Meier: none of them returned from the extermination camps in the east.

Postscript

by Marion Neiss

The Berlin memorial book devoted to Jewish victims of National Socialism contains the names of Beer (Boris) and Feiga (Fanja) Schönhaus, transported to 'the east' on 13 June 1942. The date of Boris Schönhaus's death is recorded as 16 August 1942; the place, Majdanek. Fanja Schönhaus, née Berman, is stated to have disappeared in Majdanek.

Lublin-Majdanek concentration camp was situated in the so-called Generalgouvernement, in German-occupied Poland, and was originally designated as 'the Waffen-SS prisoner-of-war camp, Lublin'. Its construction began in the autumn of 1941. In the course of 1942/43 the camp received Jewish and non-Jewish Poles, as well as Jews from Czechoslovakia and Slovenia, from the ghettos of Warsaw and Bialystok, and from the territory of the Reich. By the end of 1942, when the construction of the gas chambers in Lublin-Majdanek was completed, Zyklon B was being used to murder prisoners immediately upon arrival. On one day alone, 3 November 1943, 17,000 prisoners were shot in Majdanek. The action was triggered by the revolt of prisoners in the more easterly extermination camp of Sobibor on 14 October 1943. For fear of similar outbreaks in other camps, orders were given under the codename 'Operation Harvest Festival' to shoot Jews in the Trawniki work camp near Lublin-Majdanek and in other prison camps. In all, this action accounted for some 43,000 Jewish lives. Majdanek was liberated in July 1944. About 200,000 people died there, 60,000 to 80,000 of them Jews.

Boris and Fanja Schönhaus were deported in June 1942 to Lublin-Majdanek concentration and extermination camp on the fifteenth transport sent there from Berlin. The postcard that Boris Schönhaus managed to smuggle out to his son suggests that the couple lost touch with each other on the journey or immediately after arrival in the camp.

Aunt Sophie and Uncle Meier Berman were deported to Theresienstadt on 22 September 1942, and from there to Auschwitz. Both are recorded as missing. Enta (Marie) Berman, Cioma Schönhaus's beloved 'Grandma', was taken to Theresienstadt on 3 October 1942, and died there on 3 February 1943.

Boris and Fanja Schönhaus had come to Berlin in the early 1920s. Boris had deserted from the Red Army; he and his wife were looking for a new and better life. They belonged to the large group of Russian émigrés driven out of the country by civil war and the Revolution. At the beginning of the twenties the Russian community in Berlin numbered close to 300,000. Among the political exiles – monarchists, socialists and conservatives – there was also a large colony of artists, intellectuals and writers, turning Berlin in the early years of the Weimar Republic into a centre of Russian art and culture. But the refugees fleeing from Soviet Russia included stateless persons, the politically persecuted and displaced, vagrants, victims of financial ruin, and people escaping the famine in the Volga Basin, Ukraine and Belarus. Among those washed up in the flood of homeless people were Eastern European Jews who had managed to escape from the pogroms in Poland, Ukraine and Belarus. Affluent Russians settled in the western part of Berlin, and the less well-off – including Cioma Schönhaus's parents – moved into the Alexanderplatz area, in what is known as the 'Scheunenviertel' (literally 'the barn quarter').

Fanja and Boris Schönhaus both came from Minsk, in Belarus. Fanja had already settled in Berlin with her family when Boris Schönhaus quit his unit to follow her. They were

Me with my parents, Boris and Fanja Schönhaus-Berman. I was born in Berlin on 28 September 1922 as Samson Schönhaus. My pet name was Cioma.

married in 1920 in Berlin, and Boris attempted to find a living. The Jewish settlement of Palestine was being promoted by Zionist circles he probably met among the Eastern European Jews in Berlin. Inspired by Zionism, Boris Schönhaus decided to emigrate to Palestine. In 1926 the couple settled with their son Cioma, just four years old, in Rishon LeZion. Rishon LeZion was the first agricultural colony in Palestine; lying to the south of the port of Jaffa, it was founded in 1882 by Russian settlers. With 2,000 settlers, their vineyards already flourishing alongside grain crops, almond and orange trees, and with the biggest winemaking plant in the country, Rishon LeZion was well established.

But like so many immigrants, Fanja and Boris Schönhaus could not adapt to the climate, or to the extremely spartan living conditions in Palestine. After only a year, and influenced by the lack of reliable medical care when their now five-year-old son Cioma fell ill, they decided to return to

Europe. The Schönhaus family went back to Berlin, moving into Sophienstrasse. Boris Schönhaus started up a mineral water bottling plant, which brought the family a steady income. They were granted only a few years in which to enjoy a secure living and a middle-class lifestyle in Berlin.

Fanja and Boris had not only found asylum in Germany, but hoped to put down roots there. Both admired German literature and art, and internalized the so-called Prussian virtues. They felt that the nationalists' anti-Semitic hate campaigns, already in evidence during the Weimar Republic, could be overcome. Like so many Jews in Germany, Fanja and Boris Schönhaus could not believe that a Nazi regime might represent a mortal danger. Again like many German Jews, they looked on sombrely and anxiously as the Nazis seized power on 30 January 1933, but sought solace in the supposed German tradition of law and order. This was stressed, too, by the Central Association of German Citizens of the Jewish Faith in its official publication: 'Now as ever, Jews in Germany will maintain the calm that comes from awareness of their indestructible ties to everything that is truly German. Less than ever before will they allow their inner attitude to Germany to be affected by external attacks which they feel are unjust. They are far too deeply conscious of what this German realm means to them.'

The boycott announced by the NSDAP and carried out on 1 April 1933, calling on the public to avoid Jewish shops, doctors and lawyers, and to bar Jews from schools and universities, came as a great shock but did not lead to a general, panic-induced exodus. Of the roughly 500,000 Jews in Germany, about 37,000 left the country in 1933. Even when conditions for Jews deteriorated increasingly as a result of discriminatory laws and decrees, the number of émigrés never exceeded 25,000 a year. It was not until 1938, after the November pogroms when synagogues and

Jewish businesses were destroyed and torched, that their numbers rose to 40,000, and to 78,000 by 1939. In total, only about half of all the 500,000 Jews in Germany succeeded in fleeing abroad.

Nor did Cioma's parents consider emigrating. For one thing, where would they go? For another, they lacked the necessary means. As Cioma's account shows, 'evacuation' to the east was viewed with anxiety, but not entirely without a degree of composure. The idea of evading deportation orders by going into hiding was entirely alien to Boris and Fanja Schönhaus, as it was to many of their co-religionists.

By the end of 1941 there were about 73,000 Jews living in Berlin. Many had only arrived in the capital in recent years, seeking safety from anti-Semitic discrimination in the anonymity of the metropolis, and deluding themselves that the presence of Jewish organizations with their headquarters in the city would afford them protection from persecution and deprivation of rights. Many who had decided to emigrate came to Berlin hoping to ease their passage abroad by making direct contact with foreign embassies and agencies. When emigration was banned on 23 October 1941, however, that hope too was dashed; a few days earlier, the first Jews had been deported from Berlin to the Lodz ghetto.

Jews now had only two choices: either escape abroad illegally, or defy deportation orders by going underground. Only a few had the courage to go into hiding: life as a 'U-Boot' (submarine), as they called themselves, meant attempting to survive without a secure abode, without ration coupons and without identity papers. At a conservative estimate some 10,000 Jews in Germany attempted to go underground, about half of them in Berlin. There as elsewhere, those who dared to take this step were dependent on the help of others. Such assistance might vary greatly, extending from organizing food provision to sheltering fugitive Jews, or even, as Cioma

Schönhaus reports, acquiring identity papers and forging them. However, most Jews living underground in Berlin possessed neither false nor genuine papers, but hustled from one hiding place to another. Aside from finding shelter for the night, there were also the daylight hours to deal with. Where could you spend the day without arousing suspicion, without being recognized? Many people in hiding wandered aimlessly through the streets of Berlin, spent their time in parks and cemeteries, or mixed with passers-by in the big squares. Men in hiding were at greater risk on the city scene than women, because males of military age out of uniform soon attracted identity checks. That was why many men who had found longer-term accommodation never left their boltholes for days at a time, but only occasionally emerged at night to creep through the streets. Women and children living with their helpers had somewhat more freedom of movement, and if anyone asked questions they could be passed off as relatives or friends.

Of course, helpers were also exposed to the risk of discovery. Over-vigilant neighbours or zealous Nazis might report their suspicions to the authorities, so that the external threat was ever-present, for helpers as well as for those in hiding. But there were often internal difficulties, too. Life at close quarters and the dependence of each party on the other could lead to purely human conflicts. Often, quarrels became so bitter that fugitives were forced to leave secure hideouts and look for new ones. Intimate living could also lead to the opposite situation, such as a love affair which left a third member of the household out in the cold, and thus represented a danger. Even where relative harmony prevailed in shared accommodation, the sudden illness of a fugitive could lead to serious problems. In such cases particularly, the helpers in their turn were thrown back upon on a wider circle of collaborators who could bring in a doctor or a nurse to take care of the patient. Disaster threatened if an illegal protégé died in one's home. What to do with the body of the deceased? In extremis, the corpse would be taken under shelter of darkness to a park bench, in the hope that it would be found and buried anonymously: everything that might indicate the dead person's identity or their last abode had to be emptied from pockets.

Constant fear dogged both parties, exacerbated from spring 1943 onwards by the Gestapo's appointment of 'Jewish stalkers' to find and denounce Jews living illegally in Berlin. Stella Goldschlag, mentioned by Cioma Schönhaus, was not the only one to instil fear in Jewish fugitives. In Berlin the Gestapo recruited about twenty '*Greifer*' ('snatchers' or 'catchers'), as they were called by underground Jews. Pressurized by the authorities, and in return for vague promises that they and their families would be exempt from deportation, they embarked on their spying careers. It is not known how many Jews were betrayed by these *Greifer* in Berlin. However, according to eyewitness estimates, Stella Goldschlag alone was responsible for the arrest of about a hundred people. It is true that she and other informers also saved people from deportation by warning those they cared for that raids were imminent. But the Jewish *Greifer* had limited room for manoeuvre, since they were under constant surveillance by the Gestapo, and if they were caught helping anyone, they or their families faced inevitable deportation.

However, the greatest danger came from the ordinary population, which slavishly served the Nazi regime. The commonest motives for denouncing Jews to the authorities were envy, excessive zeal in obeying orders, or sheer malice. The latter motive must have been behind the missive that broke up the group of collaborators around Dr Franz Kaufmann in the summer of 1943:

Urgent. Jewish matter.

Wish to make an important communication to you concerning a Jewess. I have noticed for some time that people are hiding a Jewess in this building, she does not wear a star.

The Jewess is called Blumenfeld, and she is being secretly hidden [sic] by Frau Reichert, Berlin W., 39 Passauer Strasse, 3 floors up, front building. This must be stopped immediately, send an official straight away about 7 in the morning to pick this woman up.

When this Jewess lived in the building before she was always cheeky and stuck up. But you will have to be quick because otherwise she might disappear and go somewhere else.

Heil Hitler

This letter was received on 7 August 1943 at Gestapo Office IV D 1 in Berlin. Five days later, on Thursday 12 August, 49-year-old Lotte Blumenfeld – who had been a fugitive from deportation since January 1943 – was arrested in Passauer Strasse. She could not validate her claim to be a Slovak citizen, and eventually confessed that she was in contact with a man who was going to provide her with a Slovak passport – a fake one, of course. As a result of her statement, this intermediary was arrested the same day. He was serving as a reserve station sergeant in the police force at the time. Under interrogation, he too named the contacts from whom he had obtained false papers. Thereupon, on 14 August, 59-year-old Leon Blum was arrested. During questioning he confessed to having provided fugitive Jews with forged papers, which he had obtained from former Chief Secretary Franz Kaufmann, of No. 3 Hobrechtstrasse, Berlin-Halensee.

When the Gestapo arrived shortly afterwards at 3

Hobrechtstrasse to arrest Franz Kaufmann, he had already fled to go into hiding with friends. The house was immediately placed under observation, and on 18 August Ernst Hallermann, one of Kaufmann's collaborators, was arrested there. His statement led to the arrest of Kaufmann, just a day later in the open street in the Moabit district of Berlin. When picked up, he was carrying a notebook containing the names, addresses and telephone numbers of Jews living underground, as well as those of his contacts and other collaborators. Under Gestapo interrogation Kaufmann was forced to divulge the names of other underground Jews, who were arrested a few days later. The circle of those arrested expanded daily, drawing in some fifty people by early October 1943, the majority of them Jews.

Eleven of those arrested, so-called Aryans and half-breeds, were charged in November 1943 with crimes against the war economy regulations and with forging documents. Ernst Hallermann was sentenced to eight years' imprisonment, and the others received lesser sentences.

Franz Kaufmann remained under arrest until these sentences were pronounced in January 1944; no charges were laid against him, since as a Jew he was no longer subject to the law, but only to police power. On 17 February 1944 he was taken to Sachsenhausen concentration camp, and promptly shot.

The course of Kaufmann's life history was consistent and undeviating until 1936: he was the model of a correct Prussian civil servant. Born to Jewish parents in 1886 and baptized a Protestant, he served during the First World War in the 10th Bavarian Field Artillery Regiment, receiving the Iron Cross First and Second Class, the Bavarian Military Order of Merit Fourth Class with Crossed Swords, and the Frontline Service Cross. After being wounded, he was discharged from the army in 1918 as a reserve lieutenant. Having obtained his doctorate in law and political science, in 1922 he was appointed briefly to a specialist post in local government finances in the Prussian Ministry of the Interior, and selected in the same year by Charlottenburg Borough Council as a city councillor. However, Kaufmann declined the offer, preferring to take up an appointment as Chief Secretary in the Reich Finance Ministry. In 1928 he moved on to the Reich Public Accounts Office. In 1936, because of his Jewish origins, he was dismissed – or, as the minutes of his interrogation put it, 'superannuated'. In keeping with his qualifications, he then devoted himself to private study of the development of independent local government. When war broke out in 1939 he immediately volunteered for service in the forces and the Red Cross. But these efforts came to nothing, and from the middle of 1940 onwards he linked up with a Bible-study group of the Confessing Church.

In 1942, Kaufmann was drafted into forced labour. His job was to repair damaged army water canteens. Hence the reference in the Gestapo minutes to 'Franz Kaufmann, Chief Secretary, re-trained as labourer'.

It was now that he began to supply post-office ID cards to fugitive Jews. Some were acquired through members of the Confessing Church, some from other intermediaries, and some – to quote the Gestapo minutes – 'occasionally turned up' at his home. He then moved on to the provision of identity cards issued by various concerns – AEG, Telefunken, Borsig and Siemens – as well as certificates of Aryan descent, food ration cards, household identification cards (to be presented each time ration cards were issued), ID cards for drawing upon special local supplies, ID cards for personnel of the German Work Front and for employees of the BVG (Berlin Transport Company), and driving licences. From the beginning of 1943 Ernst Hallermann – arrested when Kaufmann's home was under surveillance – was responsible for buying in genuine papers or blank identity documents, while Cioma Schönhaus undertook the forging of papers.

Chief Secretary Franz Kaufmann, a conscientious and loyal servant of the state until his dismissal, set out the reasons for his actions:

'My deep roots in a Christian standpoint, and my mature years, have no doubt given me a heightened awareness of the need and suffering that can afflict the individual more or less through no fault of his own. That made me, unintentionally, a focus and meeting point for Jewish fugitives. I could not disappoint their trust and their hope that I could help them, including giving emotional support. I offered my help not because they were Jews, but because they were people, in need and afraid. For preference, the same drive to help inclined me to direct my efforts elsewhere, e.g. to the medical orderly service, for which I volunteered at the beginning of the war, but in vain; I would have been as eager to serve there as I was as a soldier in the World War.'

The hope and confidence that Franz Kaufmann gave to so many persecuted people was destroyed by that letter of denunciation on 7 August 1943. The intermediate report of Gestapo Office IV D 1 reads: 'The Jews arrested in connection with this case have already been deported if no longer needed for the case, or the State Police have taken steps to deal with them.'

Leon Blum died as early as 9 September 1943 – allegedly from a heart attack – in the Jewish Hospital; a Jewish woman killed herself in custody; and the Jews who were caught were deported to the east. A single denunciation led to the deaths of at least twenty-six people. They were murdered or lost in Auschwitz, Minsk and Kovno. Among them was Lotte Blumenfeld.

About 1,500 Jews living underground in Berlin saw out the end of the war.

Notes

1 The Reich Representation of German Jews (*Reichsvertretung der deutschen Juden*) represented Jews in their dealings with the Reich authorities. Among its responsibilities were Jewish schools and education, economic aid, welfare at work, social support, and oversight of external and internal migration. In March 1938 it lost its status as a body incorporated under public law, and could therefore no longer raise taxes. In June 1939 the organization was re-named 'Association of Jews in Germany' (*Reichsvereinigung der Juden in Deutschland*: note that Jews were no longer German Jews, but 'Jews in Germany'), and all Jewish organizations still extant were incorporated into it. It was also subject to control by the Reich minister of the interior, and obliged to follow his directives, including deportation preparations. In 1943 the office of the Reich Association was dissolved; its assets were seized, and its remaining staff members sent to concentration camps.

Until 23 June 1941 the Schlosshofstrasse work camp near Bielefeld functioned as a re-training camp to prepare for emigration. It then became simply a work camp for Jews deployed as labourers by the municipal authorities. See Margit Naarmann, *Die Paderborner Juden 1802–1945*, Paderborn 1988.

2 On 10 May 1933 so-called book-burning ceremonies took place in all the university towns of the German Reich, where books by authors guilty of an 'un-German spirit' were consigned to the flames. Among the numerous banned authors were Thomas Mann, Karl Marx, Erich Kästner and Kurt Tucholsky. *Die Weltbühne* (The World Stage) was a celebrated left-wing magazine featuring political, economic and cultural articles. Its famous editors were Kurt Tucholsky and Carl von Ossietzky.

3 In 1941 the Secret State Police (*Geheime Staatspolizei*, or Gestapo) had sixty-seven offices in the German Reich. Within these offices there were various departments covering e.g. Party affairs, press/literary/cultural policies, economics etc. The activities of the 'Jewish Affairs Department' (*Judenreferat*) within the Gestapo extended from the supervision and regulation of Jewish community life, the establishment of 'racial identity', and ensuring that the anti-Jewish laws were observed, to the organization of deportations. Pützer was head of the Jewish department in the Bielefeld Gestapo branch office, which from 1941 onwards came under the authority of the Gestapo office in Münster. See Joachim Meynert, 'Das Ende vor Augen. Die Deportation der Juden aus Bielefeld', in *Verfolgung und Widerstand im Rheinland und Westfalen 1933–1945*, ed. by Anselm Faust, Cologne, 1992, pp. 162–74.

4 The well-known writer had a Jewish wife, who had two daughters from an earlier marriage. Jochen Klepper was excluded from the Reich Writers' Chamber, and because of his marriage to a Jewess was declared 'unworthy to serve' in the forces. His elder stepdaughter, Brigitte, succeeded in emigrating to Britain in 1939. When his younger stepdaughter received her deportation summons in December 1942, the couple and their daughter committed suicide.

5 The Berolina statue in the Alexanderplatz was a pre-war Berlin landmark, a colossal, motherly female figure in bronze.

6 A statutory regulation incorporated in the Reich Citizens' Law of 27 September 1938 excluded Jewish lawyers from the German bar. The legal administration authorities permitted so-called Jewish advisers (*Konsulenten*) to provide guidance and representation for Jewish clients.

7 A directive of 21 September 1940 decreed that special air-raid shelters had to be built for Jews.

8 The Three Power Pact of September 1940 committed Italy, Germany and Japan to come to each other's aid in the case of attack by the USA. After the Japanese launched their surprise assault on the US fleet on 7/8 December 1941 at Pearl Harbor on the Hawaiian island of Oahu, Germany and Italy declared war on the USA on 11 December 1941.

9 According to the 'Law for the protection of German blood and German honour' (*Gesetz zum Schutz des deutschen Blutes und der deutschen Ehre*, also known as the 'Nuremberg Laws') people with one Jewish grandparent were classed as 'mixed race of the second degree', and those with two Jewish grandparents as 'mixed race of the first degree'. All men of military age in both categories were called up, but until 1942 those of 'mixed race of the first degree' were then discharged. Men of 'mixed race of the second degree' had to produce special reasons to justify their remaining in the forces.

10 From 1 January 1941 onwards Jewish men were compelled to add 'Israel' to their name, and women 'Sara'.

11 From 15 September 1941 onwards all Jews over the age of six had to wear a yellow star on a black background visibly displayed on the upper part of their clothing.

12 A curfew was imposed on Jews from 1 September 1939. They were forbidden to leave their homes after 20.00 in winter and 21.00 in summer.

13 The decree of 13 November 1941 banned Jews from using bicycles.

14 See the detailed account by Winfried Meyer in *Unternehmen Sieben. Eine Rettungsaktion für vom Holocaust Bedrohte aus dem Amt Ausland/Abwehr im Oberkommando der Wehrmacht*, Frankfurt am Main, 1993.

15 The law banning Jews from emigrating from the German Reich was passed on 23 October 1941.

16 By a decree of 18 September 1941 Jews could only use public transport under strictly limited conditions, and on 24 April 1942 they were barred from it altogether, with the exception of Jewish forced labourers, who were issued with permits for travel to work.

17 Regulation 11 of the Reich Citizens' Law of 25 November 1941 stated that any Jew moving abroad should forfeit his estate to the Reich. A confidential circular of 3 December 1941 extended these powers to apply to Jews 'resettled' in territories occupied by German troops, especially the Generalgouvernement and Ukraine.

18 The 'Leibstandarte Adolf Hitler' was founded in March 1933 as

a 120-man-strong bodyguard. They swore an oath to Hitler personally, and were outside the constitutional framework of state and party. They were initially responsible for ceremonial and security duties and the personal protection of Hitler, but in 1939 they were incorporated into the Waffen-SS.

19 Hassidism is an orthodox movement within Judaism.

20 Majdanek was a concentration and extermination camp in the Lublin district of Majdan Tatarski, in the Generalgouvernement. Construction of the camp began in late 1941, and it served mainly to hold Soviet prisoners-of-war in transit. From September 1942, Jewish and non-Jewish Poles and Jews from Czechoslovakia and Slovenia were sent there. The construction of the gas chambers was concluded by November 1942. At least 200,000 people were murdered in Majdanek, about 60,000–80,000 of them Jews.

21 Theresienstadt was an Austrian fortress town in northern Bohemia, founded in 1780. From 1941, after the non-Jewish population had been evacuated, Jews from Bohemia and Moravia were interned there. From 1942 mainly elderly and infirm Jews were brought to the so-called old-age ghetto of Theresienstadt. Jews deported to Theresienstadt were obliged to sign 'home purchase contracts', by which they surrendered their estate in return for 'care and board'. Over 140,000 Jews were deported to Theresienstadt. For 88,000 people the 'old-age ghetto' was only a transit stage en route to another concentration and extermination camp. About 33,500 people died in Theresienstadt.

22 Thesi Goldstadt was married to a Jew. The marriage of a Jewish husband to an Aryan wife counted as a 'privileged mixed marriage' as long as it produced a child who did not adhere to the Jewish religious community. If the Goldschmidts had not had a child, their marriage would not have enjoyed 'privileged' status. The marriage of an Aryan man to a Jewish wife was 'privileged', even if there were no children of the marriage. A couple in a mixed marriage were regarded as 'non-privileged' if their offspring were observing Jews.

23 See note 9.

24 Since August 1936 Ernst von Weizsäcker had been head of the political department of the Foreign Office, and its under-secretary

of state since March 1938. From June 1943 to 1945 he was German ambassador to the Vatican.

25 Erhard Milch became Chief of Staff of the *Luftwaffe* in 1939. His supposed Jewish origins were overlooked in the forces.

26 Karin Hardt and Hans Albers were famous actors.

27 A decree of 13 March 1942 ordered that the doorways of Jewish dwellings must be marked with a star.

28 Dr Franz Kaufmann was a Jew baptized as a Protestant, with a non-Jewish wife. Because of his Jewish origins, in 1936 he was dismissed from his post as chief secretary. He was arrested for his illegal activities in 1943, and murdered in Sachsenhausen concentration camp in 1944.

29 The Confessing Church (*Bekennende Kirche*, or BK) was set up in opposition to the German Christians (*Deutsche Christen*, or DC), who were organizationally and ideologically aligned with Nazism. The BK was not strictly a movement of political resistance to National Socialism, whose legitimacy it did not basically question. None the less, some parishes and individuals did openly oppose the regime, or supported political resistance.

30 Johannes Blaskowitz was General Officer commanding the 8th Army in the Polish campaign, and Commander in Chief East. Blaskowitz was deprived of his command in May 1940 because of his protests about SS excesses, but a few months later he was appointed General Officer commanding 1st Army, France.

31 Werner Scharff (1912–45) was a member of the resistance group 'Community for Peace and Reconstruction' (*Gemeinschaft für Frieden und Aufbau*). He was arrested in 1944, and shot in March 1945 in Sachsenhausen concentration camp.

32 'Post-office identity cards' became increasingly common in the course of the war. People who were bombed out and lost their papers could apply for an identity card (*Postausweis*) in any post-office branch. As the chaos of war intensified from 1943 onwards, it became ever more difficult for the authorities to check the information on such provisional documents.

33 A 'Berlin room' was a typical feature of the big Berlin tenements built in the nineteenth century. Having a window facing on to

the inner courtyard, it was dark, and it linked the front building to a side wing of the complex.

34 A childless mixed marriage was only 'privileged' if the husband was a non-Jew.

35 Gustav Gründgens and Käthe Gold were famous actors.

36 Renate Klepper was the stepdaughter of the author Jochen Klepper. Klepper's Jewish wife had two daughters from a previous marriage. The elder daughter, Brigitte, succeeded in emigrating in time. When Renate Klepper received her deportation order, the family committed suicide on 11 December 1942.

37 This was the 'Russian Commission in Germany' (*Russische Vertrauensstelle in Deutschland*), which operated under National Socialist supervision. The purpose of the *Vertrauensstelle* was to issue identity documents to all Russian immigrants over fifteen which served to legitimize them in their dealings with the various authorities responsible for aliens. The Commission also functioned like a consulate, but under Gestapo control. See Bettina Dodenhoeft and Vasilij von Biskupskij, 'Eine Emigrantenkarriere in Deutschland', in Karl Schlögel (ed.), *Russische Emigration in Deutschland 1918 bis 1942*, Berlin 1995, pp. 219–28.

38 Johannes Popitz (1884–1945) was Prussian Minister of Finance from 1933 to 1944. As a member of the conservative resistance group around Carl Goerdeler he was arrested after the failure of the plot to assassinate Hitler on 20 July 1944, and executed in February 1945.

39 The three short notes and one long one which open Beethoven's Fifth Symphony echo the Morse code for V, which stood for 'victory'. The V sound on drums became the wartime call sign for all of the BBC's European services. The BBC had a policy of neutral reporting of Allied disasters as well as successes, and of avoiding overt bias and propaganda, so that its reports tended to be believed even by Germans. 'Enemy listening', as it was called, was punishable by death in Germany, but none the less millions of Germans tuned in clandestinely to BBC news broadcasts.

40 Gertrud Staewen and Etta von Oertzen were members of the Confessing Church.

41 Karl Barth (1886–1968) was a theologian who paved the way intellectually for the Confessing Church.

42 The Protestant theologian Martin Niemöller, a famous submarine captain in the First World War, was arrested in 1937 for sermons criticizing the regime, and deported to Sachsenhausen and Dachau concentration camps. He survived the war.

43 Heinrich Brüning was a member of the Zentrum (mainly Catholic) Party, and Reich Chancellor from 1930 to 1932. In 1934 he fled to the USA via the Netherlands, and in 1939 was appointed professor at Harvard University.

44 Being of so-called mixed race, Ernst Hallermann was not eligible to serve in the forces. He was arrested when the group around Franz Kaufmann was exposed, and he remained in Brandenburg Prison until 1945.

45 From 1949 onwards, with the foundation of the Federal Republic of Germany, efforts were made by West Germany to compensate those who had suffered at the hands of the National Socialist regime. Various attempts at legislation to regulate claims and payments were incorporated in the Federal Indemnification (or Compensation) Law, the *Bundesentschädigungsgesetz* of 1956. Restitution cases were dealt with in various regional offices, including Berlin, and by their nature involved complex administration. Helene Jacobs was professionally associated with the Berlin Compensation Office (*Entschädigungsamt Berlin*). For the rest of her life she lived on in Berlin in the flat where she had sheltered Cioma Schönhaus, at No. 2 Bonner Strasse, Wilmersdorf. There is now a plaque commemorating her at the entrance to the building.

46 In Gustav Schwab's nineteenth-century ballad, 'The Ride across Lake Constance', a horseman who has just ridden across the frozen lake learns on the other side that the ice is nowhere more than half an inch thick: the shock makes him fall from his horse, and he dies.

47 The reference here is surely not to the election of March 1933, by which time Hitler had already become Reich Chancellor, but none the less the Nazis gained 'only' 43.9% of the vote, and no absolute majority. The vote referred to here is the result in the elections of 12 November 1933, which also incorporated a

plebiscite on Germany's withdrawal from the League of Nations. Only one party was now contesting the elections, but even so the official results (95.11% in the plebiscite, 92.1% in the 'Reichstag election') can be seen as an overwhelming endorsement for Hitler, indicating that he had the support of a large majority of the nation. This was certainly the perception in Germany and elsewhere at the time. Further votes before the war produced similar 'positive' results.

48 The allusion is to the so-called 'Day of Potsdam' in 1933, the ceremonial opening of the new, Nazi-dominated, Reichstag in Potsdam on 21 March – a date chosen to commemorate the opening of the first Reichstag following Bismarck's foundation of the Second Reich in 1871: 'The Garnisonkirche (garrison church) in Potsdam, where the main ceremony was to take place, had been founded by the Hohenzollern kings of Prussia in the early eighteenth century. Household guards had dedicated themselves there to service to God and the King. Frederick Wilhelm I, the "Soldier King", and his son Frederick the Great were buried in the crypt. The church symbolized the bonds between the Prussian military, monarchy, the power of the state, and the Protestant religion . . . Dressed not in party uniform but in a dark morning-suit [Hitler] played the part of the humble servant, bowing deeply before the revered and elderly Reich President [Hindenburg] and offering him his hand.' (Ian Kershaw, *Hitler. 1889–1936: Hubris*, London 1998, p. 465.)

49 Otto Skorzeny was a member of the 'Leibstandarte Adolf Hitler' (see note 18), and he planned and led the action to rescue Benito Mussolini.

50 Benito Mussolini, founder of the Italian Fascist Party (PNF), became Prime Minister in 1922, and dictator ('Il Duce') from 1925. In July 1943 the Fascist Grand Council deposed him, and he was arrested and interned.

Die Nacht ist wild

Die Victor wird
nie gefragt, ob er
die Wahrheit sagte!